# DEVELOPING ORGANIZATIONS:
# DIAGNOSIS AND ACTION

PAUL R. LAWRENCE
*Harvard University*

JAY W. LORSCH
*Harvard University*

ADDISON-WESLEY PUBLISHING COMPANY
Reading, Massachusetts • Menlo Park, California
London • Amsterdam • Don Mills, Ontario • Sydney

This book is in the Addison-Wesley series:

ORGANIZATION DEVELOPMENT

Editors
Edgar Schein
Warren Bennis
Richard Beckhard

ISBN 0-201-04204-5
NOPQRSTUVW-DO-89876543210

To Our Wives

# FOREWORD

The purpose of this common foreword to all the volumes of the Addison-Wesley Series on Organization Development is twofold: (1) to give the reader some idea as to the origin and purpose of the series; and (2) to guide the reader through the content of the different books.

The series came to be because we felt there was a growing theory and practice of something called "organization development," but most students, colleagues, and managers knew relatively little about it. Many of us are highly active as OD consultants, but little has been written about what we do when we are with a client or what our underlying theory of consultation is. We were also acutely aware of the fact that, though there are common assumptions shared by most practitioners of OD, there are great individual variations in the strategies and tactics employed by different consultants. The field is still emerging and new methods are constantly being invented. It seemed appropriate, therefore, not to try to write a single text, but to give several of the foremost theorist-practitioners a chance to explain their own view of OD and their own style of working with client systems.

The authors of this series of six books represent a variety of points of view, but they do not exhaust the major approaches currently in use in OD. There are some obvious names missing—Argyris, Tannenbaum, Ferguson, Bradford, Davis, Burke—to name just a few. We hope in future volumes of the series to get these men and others to write about their theory and practice.

The six books of this series can be described as follows: Bennis presents a very broad survey of the history and present practice of OD. How and why did it come about, what is it, and what are some of the major unresolved issues in OD? The Beckhard volume is a systematic attempt to describe the various strategies and tactics employed in different kinds of OD efforts. Beckhard goes beyond his own approach and tries to build a general framework within which most OD programs can be located. The Beckhard and Bennis volumes together give the reader an excellent overview of the field.

The two volumes by Blake and Mouton and by Lawrence and Lorsch are somewhat more personalized statements of their particular views of how organizations function, how organizational excellence is to be judged, and how an OD effort can contribute to the achievement of such excellence. Both books are focused on total organization systems and attempt to show how intervention in organizations leads to constructive change and development.

The volumes by Walton and Schein are written at a more specific level. They highlight some of the day-to-day activities of the consultant as he works with a client system in the context of an OD program. Both deal with the process of the consultation itself. In the Walton book the focus is on the process by which the consultant uses himself to aid in the resolution of conflict. In the Schein book the idea of "process consultation" is introduced and explained in detail. The kinds of organizational processes which are described in these last two volumes lie at the heart of OD efforts, but the focus of the books is on the moment-to-moment behavior of the consultant rather than the overall design of the OD program.

The six books were written independently with only broad guidelines and minimum coordination by the editors. It was our hope and intention to get six very personal and unique statements, rather than a closely integrated set of "chapters." We feel that the amount of overlap is minimal, and that the books in fact complement each other very well in being written at different levels of generality. We hope that the reader will sense that the field of OD is converging toward common theories and practices, but that we are a long way from being able to produce a definitive "text" on the subject.

*March 1969*                                         Edgar H. Schein
                                                     Richard Beckhard
                                                     Warren G. Bennis

# PREFACE

This book represents a personal statement of our evolving experience as collaborators in the work of developing organizations. The methods which we describe in this small volume had their origins in an extensive line of research on which we have collaborated over about seven years.[1] Our consulting work is, therefore, rather uniquely rooted in a major research effort.

In following our research leads, we have been concerned with a wide range of organizational problems, but they have focused on three critical interfaces; the organization-environment interface; the group-group interface; and the individual-organization interface. In exploring these three kinds of relations, we have paid close attention to the attainment both of organizational goals and of individual purpose. We have dealt both with structural variables and with process elements. We have consistently emphasized a sequence of intervention in which diagnosis precedes action planning. Also emphasized is the notion that organizations can usefully be conceived of as systems. The power of this set of ideas is that it can be

1   The joint publications by the authors that have been a direct product of this research are: *Organization and Environment*, Division of Research, Graduate School of Business, Harvard University, 1967; "New management job: The integrator," *Harv. Bus. Rev.*, November-December 1967; "Differentiation and integration in complex organizations," *Admin. Sci. Quart.*, 12, No. 1, June 1967; and "Organizing for product innovation," *Harv. Bus. Rev.*, November-December 1964.

adapted in a flexible but consistent manner to local problems and opportunities.

As in all such matters, it is difficult to offer "proof" of the effectiveness of our approach to organization development. We and our clients in organizations have found it helpful in solving their problems. Perhaps the best test for the reader is whether he finds that this approach helps him better understand his own experiences with otherwise complex organizational issues, and whether he can visualize its successful application to such issues.

The book is arranged to present first our overview of organization development and a summary of the research on which it is based. We then proceed to examine issues at each of the three critical interfaces, presenting brief examples of work on each. Finally, the concluding chapter pulls these themes together in a set of conclusions about organization development issues as they present themselves to practicing managers.

In presenting the material in this book, we want to acknowledge our indebtedness to a number of people. George Litwin, our colleague in organizational behavior, has contributed his ideas and his experience in an important consulting relationship. In addition, we have drawn on the research of, and collaborated with, Louis Barnes and Larry Greiner. Ken Benne contributed his efforts and his wisdom to one of the consulting engagements reported. Two of our doctoral students, John Morse and Jack Gabarro, have helped in generous measure on aspects of the case studies we used as examples. We are indebted to Mrs. Ann Walter and Miss Jeanne Deschamps for typing the several drafts and for editorial help. Finally, the companies and their executives with whom we have worked, though they must remain anonymous, are acknowledged as key contributors to our growing understanding of the process by which organization improvement can be achieved.

*January 1969*                                                          P.R.L.
                                                                        J.W.L.

# CONTENTS

# 1
# INTRODUCTION

Practicing managers and students of administration are besieged with ideas about and techniques for improving the effectiveness of their organization. For example, in the area of decision-making they are told on the one hand to encourage more autonomy and participation in decision-making by organization members at all levels of the hierarchy. On the other hand, they are advised to rely more heavily on the computer and/or programmatic decision techniques, such as PERT, to improve the decision-making effectiveness of their organization. Similarly, in the area of motivation, they are advised by some authorities that money is still a powerful incentive and by others that money is really not a motivator at all. With regard to the structure of the organization, they are advised by some authors and consultants to delegate authority and responsibility equally and to keep the chain of command clear, while other authorities suggest that organization structures should have more of a "free form" or "organic" characteristic.

These are just a sample of the issues on which such apparently contradictory advice is offered to present and future managers about how to design and develop their organizations. If these human and organizational issues were only peripheral, the confusion which results would not be of much consequence; but the one point on which most practitioners, consultants, and authors do agree is that dealing with such issues is crucial to the success of an organization whether it be a business firm, a nonprofit institution, or a government agency.

This book obviously cannot unravel all the confusions and contradictions in the techniques and ideas available to deal with these human and organizational issues; but it is our intention to make a modest contribution in this direction by presenting a way of thinking which clarifies these confusions and simultaneously offers practical guidelines for management action in developing organizations. In the pages which follow, we shall try to answer several basic questions which underlie these sorts of contradictions. How can we best conceptualize organizations? What do we mean by organizational development? What are the essential relations between men and organizations and between organizations and their wider environment? Is it possible for organizations to be continuously adapting to both environmental changes and changes among their individual contributors? By what processes can this be accomplished?

In posing these questions, we should emphasize, this book will not present a synthesis of all current organizational knowledge so much as the *point of view* and the *approach* of the authors. It is in this sense that our attempt is intentionally "modest." Our point of view has grown out of both research into organizations and active consultation work directed at organizational improvement. The examples and evidence will be from both our own work and that of certain colleagues who share this point of view The concepts and methods which we will describe were selected because of their utility to us in understanding and managing the process of organizational development. They have been effective tools for us, and we feel they should also be useful to others interested in these issues. But the reader should recognize that they represent only a limited portion of the behavioral-science tools which are being developed and which can be applied to organizational development issues.

## DEFINING ORGANIZATIONS

To understand our approach, it is first necessary to state how we define organization. This means that we must start with the needs of men and why they seek to build organizations. Men must, in some way, cope with their environment. At the most general level, they start new organizations or contribute to existing ones because they thereby find *better solutions to the environmental problems* facing them. We tend to think of organizations as having a purpose, but this is not literally the case. *People* have purposes; organizations do not. A simple organization may, of course, specialize in one thing, such as the manufacture and sale of shoes. We call this its purpose, but this is acceptable only as a shorthand way of speaking. It is more accurate to say that this organization has adopted a planned strategy or goal of making and selling shoes and that this is attracting various contributions from people who are, in fact, seeking to fulfill a variety of different purposes. These people have made a common decision to work out their different purposes in a coordinated manner around the shoemaking strategy.

As organizations become more complex, we note that it is even more difficult, if not impossible, to state their "purpose" in a convenient brief statement. Who can say briefly what is the purpose of the State Department or of General Motors? If we believe that organizations have a purpose, our inability to articulate it is a disturbing experience. However, the difficulty is to be expected because the greater array of people contributing to such a complex organization will inevitably bring a greater array of complex purposes to the organization. There still remains the essential task in any organization of shaping and clarifying the central goal or goals that guide the organization's transactions with its environment. We will come back to this issue in more depth later.

Building on these ideas, we can now present a working definition of organization. *An organization is the coordination of different activities of individual contributors to carry out planned transactions with the environment.* The expression "different activities" in this definition embodies the traditional concept of division of work or, as the sociologist would say, differentiated function. If various individual contributors are going to work in an organization, they will somehow have to divide up the work; so it is descriptively accurate to make it part of our definition. The term "coordination" is the other half of the division-of-work equation. Without coordination, division of labor is random—the antithesis of organization. Organizations must have coordination to accomplish the ends outlined in their central goals. They must have at least some mechanisms for communication and decision-making before coordination can take place. This definition also reminds us, following Barnard, that people can best be thought of as contributing activities to organizations rather than being themselves totally in them.[1] The various contributors to an organization can be expected to have different degrees of personal concern about whether or not the organization as a whole is succeeding in conducting transactions with the wider environment so as to generate a

---

1    C. I. Barnard, *The Functions of the Executive*. Cambridge, Mass.: Harvard University Press, 1950.

surplus of resources and thereby to grow. This definition can be expressed symbolically as follows:

Individual $\longrightarrow$ Organization $\longrightarrow$ Wider
contributors $\longleftarrow$ (Division of work $\longleftarrow$ environment
and coordination)

The arrows indicate that the push or purpose comes from individual contributors and is fully consummated only when there are favorable transactions carried out with the wider environment.

We are now ready to use this definition to clarify what we mean by the concept of "organization development."[2] When we talk about organization development, we are implying that we want to find ways to change the organization from its current state to a better-developed state. This raises two questions which need answering before we are ready to define what we mean by organizational development. First, what are the major problem areas around which we want to change the organization? Second, how do we determine the direction in which we want to develop the organization in these areas? We now wish to deal with the first of these questions.

## ORGANIZATIONAL-DEVELOPMENT INTERFACES

Our definition of organization and, we must hasten to add, a great deal of everyday experience helps identify at least three crucial and essential developmental issues that any organization faces. It is these issues that we will explore in some depth in this book. The first of these is the process of developing the relationship or the nature of the transactions between the organization and its wider environment or what we shall call the organization-environment interface. We will refer to relationships at this interface as a "planned transaction," in order to introduce the necessary idea that there is usually a deliberate strategy which the management of an organization adopts for conducting these external transactions in a way

2    It is only in the very recent past that the term organizational development has come into general usage. It has been adopted primarily by specialists in industry who are associated with modern versions of human-relations training, such as sensitivity training. Because of the association, the term is in danger of becoming synonymous with these educational methods. Certainly this is not the intention of those who adopted the term, and we join them in seeking a much broader definition.

that promises to generate a surplus of resources for the organization. Citing some well-known examples of such strategies will clarify the point. The Ford Motor Company initiated the strategy of producing highly standardized, low-cost automobiles on the assumption that this would create a new mass market which would, in turn, enable the organization to secure the economies of large-scale production. In this instance, the planned transaction was with consumers or customers, who were the most obvious entities in the environment with whom transactions had to be made. But some organizational strategies are based more upon transactions with other elements of the environment. For example, the Aluminum Company of Canada (Alcan) was founded on the premise that a Canadian location would enable it to secure low-cost power from the undeveloped natural water resources of the area. This planned environmental transaction on the supply side constituted the unique aspect of its strategy for generating an organizational surplus in the aluminum business.

Other planned transactions might involve a unique strategy for securing capital from the money markets, or for securing technical know-how from a university source (e.g., the establishment of numerous electronic firms in the Boston area). Examples could be cited from other types of organizations such as hospitals, governmental agencies, etc.

The key developmental problem in this area, however, is not just initial strategy formulation at the time of organizational birth, but also continuing evaluation of the constant changes in the organization's relevant environment and the effect of these changes on the quality of transactions between the organization and its environment. In this book, we will not be much concerned with the issues of what the content of a strategy statement or set of goals should be for a particular firm. These issues have been covered in some detail by those interested in business policy.[3] Instead, our primary focus will be on how the quality of organization-and-environment transactions can be maintained and enhanced in the face of environmental changes.

Related to this basic issue is the proper division of activities which the organization finds necessary to carry out transactions with its environment. It is a matter of ready observation that an organization of any appreciable size must form groups or units for the performance of the different kinds of activities (tasks) that are required for the execution of its selected transactional strategy. There are several widely-used

---

3   See especially Learned, Christensen, Andrews, and Guth, *Business Policy, Text and Cases.* Homewood, Ill: Richard D. Irwin, 1965.

approaches to division of work, of which the more familiar are by task specialty or function, by geography, by product, or by time. Many ways have been found to combine these basic approaches, and there are trade-off costs and benefits associated with each.

Another issue related to maintaining the quality of transactions at the organization-and-environment interface is the extent to which each unit achieves good organizational and administrative practice, and to which its members think and behave in ways which are consistent with the transactions which must be carried out with the environment. We will have much more to say about this important issue shortly as we explore the conceptual tools we use to deal with the constellation of issues at this interface.

The necessity for each unit to have characteristics consistent with its task is directly related to the second major developmental problem we will consider—the interface among groups or units within the organization. Once organizational units are divided, as our definition of organization also suggests, the problem of achieving integration among them becomes crucial. Since groups, once formed, will evolve their own distinctive task-related characteristics, they will have different points of view that necessarily complicate the coordination process. This often generates serious intergroup problems whose symptoms are destructive competition, secretiveness, and hostility. The integration process must cope with these issues to achieve unity of effort.

We will have more to say with regard to this interface shortly, but now we want to turn to the third and final developmental issue that will be explored in this volume. It, too, is suggested by our definition of organization, and has to do with the interface between individual contributors and the organization. We have already noted that, at its inception, any organization is an expression of the purposes of its individual founders. They decide that their individual purposes can best be achieved by combining forces in an organized manner. This starts the process whereby individuals make contributions to an organization in exchange for certain inducements which they judge to be satisfactory. Once an organization is launched, its transactional strategy usually generates a need for additional contributions from people not initially associated with it. So representatives of the organization seek the services of others and negotiate agreement to secure their needed contributions. However, whether one starts his analysis with a new organization or an existing one makes no difference in terms of the requirement for a contributions-inducements agreement with individual contributors.[4] These contributors may be in roles as managers or professionals, as white- or blue-collar employees.

Many problems arise in the shifting psychological contract between man and organization. Are the parties thinking in terms of simply a job or of a career? How much emotional commitment to organizational goals is offered and expected? What balance is struck between dependence and independence, between conformity and creativity, between duty and self-expression? Is the organization accumulating a reservoir of trained human assets and good will, or is it dissipating human resources built up in an earlier period? What is being done to anticipate and provide for the talents necessary to implement new strategies attuned to environmental change?

The three general developmental issues discussed above have been selected for detailed treatment in this volume because they represent the sorts of problems we are called upon to solve as consultants. They reflect also the newer, cutting edge of organizational development work. They are not, we must emphasize, all-inclusive. Another set of major organizational-development issues with which we will not directly deal are interpersonal relations between individual contributors, whether they be superiors, subordinates, or peers, and the associated topic of the development of effective face-to-face task groups. This set of issues has already been the focus of extensive research, theorizing, and documented developmental effort. It is for these reasons only, not their relative importance, that we will not emphasize them here.

These three interfaces with which we have chosen to deal—organization-and-environment, group-to-group, and individual-and-organization, plus this fourth interface of person-to-person—represent the major problem areas in which organizational development efforts must be conducted. This discussion thus provides an answer to the first of the two questions we raised about the meaning of the term organizational development. But the second question—how to determine the desired direction for change—cannot be answered until we explore more fully some of the concepts which we utilize to work problems at these interfaces.

---

4    In using the "contributions-inducements" formulation, we will be drawing on March and Simon in *Organizations* (New York: John Wiley, 1958), pp. 84-85.

In fact, implicit in this discussion is a way of thinking which the authors have found useful in organizational studies but which now needs to be more explicit. At the most general level, it is a systems approach to the study of organization. Within this general framework is the notion of an organization as a system of differentiated units which require integration, and the view of the individual contributor as a complex problem-solving system himself. As a prelude to Chapters 3 and 4, we shall, in the next chapter, discuss the systems approach and the concepts of differentiation and integration in some detail before addressing ourselves to the question of determining the desired direction for change. We will touch only briefly here on the concept of man as a complex problem-solving system, but will deal with it more fully in Chapter 5.

# 2
## CONCEPTS FOR DEVELOPING ORGANIZATIONS

The creation of a framework for thinking about any topic such as organization development is an essential step toward understanding and action. We shall present below an interrelated set of ideas that have proved useful to us in ordering many diverse observations about organization life. They can help us make sense out of the examples that will follow and provide guidelines for application in new situations. After some brief comments on systemic analysis, we will present the concepts of differentiation and integration and relate them to our question about determining the directions for organization-development work and also to the stages of the process of organizational development.

## SYSTEMS ANALYSIS

Without attempting to spell out all the implications of a systems view of organization, we would emphasize now two crucial ideas. The first of these is the idea of an essential interdependence between the elements of the organization. In our treatment in Chapter 1 of developmental problems, we have, for purposes of simplicity, presented them as independent issues. But an organization is not a mechanical system in which one part can be changed without a concomitant effect on the other parts. Rather, an organizational system shares with biological systems the property of an intense interdependence of parts such that a change in one part has an impact on the others.[1]

For example, the activities required by a given transactional strategy, such as making shoes, can be spelled out in mechanical terms and broken into a very fine division of labor. When machines are available that can do the complete job, things might go well. But when human contributors must be engaged in the process, the situation is different. An optimal division of labor from a mechanical standpoint could generate serious costs if it is discovered that the simple repetitive work is distasteful to the available people and the inducements required to obtain their contributions become excessive.

Such examples can be cited in regard to any element of an organization. The point has been made many times, but it is especially relevant to the chapters ahead where we will be exploring these interfaces on a one-at-a-time basis, as any writer must. As human beings, the readers and the writers share a bounded rationality—we can deal in our minds with only about seven variables at a time, while the organizational world we would master is obviously much more complex. We must proceed with caution, recognizing that in treating topics one at a time, we are not recognizing all the interdependencies in organizational systems.

The second relevant critical idea deriving from systems analysis is the idea that social systems such as organizations, unlike mechanical and even biological systems, have the ability to modify themselves in basic structural ways. Buckley terms this the *morphogenic property* of organizations, and cites it as the prime identifying feature of organizations.[2] A machine cannot alter its gear train, an animal cannot develop an extra leg, but an organization can and does do analogous things. A business, a church, a bank can add or subtract new departments and

---

1    We are not suggesting that a biological system is a complete analogy for an organization. As will become apparent in a later paragraph, for example, we see organizations, unlike biological systems, as having the capacity to change their own form and structure (be morphogenic). In this regard, we share Buckley's concern that the biological view of organizations has led to inaccurate and overly pessimistic conclusions about the capacity of organization members to change the shape of their organizations. (W. Buckley, *Sociology and Modern Systems Theory*, Englewood Cliffs, N.J.: Prentice Hall, 1967.) Nevertheless, the biological analogy is useful to describe the interdependence of the parts of organizational systems.

2    Buckley, *Op. cit.*

modify its communication and authority structure. A social agency can change its constitution. This happens by a cybernetic process through which an organization's members compare the *desired* results of strategy with the *actual* results. Important discrepancies are defined as a problem and a search is undertaken for causes and remedies. Most frequently in this process some error is detected or a procedural routine is modified, but repeated discrepancies between plans and results start people exploring alternative modifications in the existing strategy and/or in the organization structure. By this feedback process, organizations literally hitch themselves along into the future.

An outsider, watching, over a period of time, the external manifestations of this process, might wrongly conclude that the organization had a long-term purpose of its own. But we now see that this is an illusion created by the viewer's point of observation. Such changes are a result, instead, of a group of individual problem-solvers identifying their welfare to a greater or lesser extent with the organizational welfare, and bringing their different purposes to a problem-solving situation on behalf of the organization. From the outside, large organizations often appear to be monolithic entities run as if by a single mastermind and moving inexorably along a predetermined path. From the inside, they frequently appear to be in a chaotic situation, trying to move in all directions at once. The truth is somewhere in between. But it is this semichaotic, semi-planned process of self-correcting and self-modifying which gives organizations the morphogenic properties that make them potentially such a flexible and powerful tool for the extension of man's control over his environment.

With this general view of organizations as highly interdependent and morphogenic systems, we want to look in detail at the concepts of differentiation and integration and how they help us understand the organization-and-environment and the group-to-group interfaces.

## THE DIFFERENTIATION-AND-INTEGRATION MODEL

The notions of differentiation and integration and associated concepts dealing with the management of intergroup conflict have been presented as a comprehensive conceptual model elsewhere.[3] We want only briefly to summarize them here. In doing so, we need to emphasize two points.

---

3    P. R. Lawrence and J. W. Lorsch, *Organization and Environment: Managing Differentiation and Integration.* Boston: Div. of Research, Harv. Bus. School, 1967.

1. The model is based on empirical study of ten organizations in three different environments. Further, these findings have been corroborated by our consulting activities in several additional settings.

2. The model is fully consistent with the view of organizations as systems. That is, instead of providing a universal prescription of the one best way to organize, it provides a framework, based on the demands of the organization's environment, by which we can understand what organizational characteristics are required if an organization is to perform effectively in its particular environment.[4]

## Differentiation

To understand the environmental demands on an organization, we start first by looking at how much differentiation should exist among the various groups. As already suggested, this depends upon what internal characteristics each group must develop to carry out planned transactions with its assigned part of the environment. More specifically, it depends primarily upon the extent to which the certainty of information within the various parts of the environment is similar or different. If these parts of the environment (e.g., the market, scientific knowledge, techno-economic or manufacturing factors) are fairly homogeneous in their degree of certainty, the units will need to be fairly similar in formal organizational practices and members' orientations. If these parts of the environment have quite different degrees of certainty, the units will need to be more differentiated. Our evidence indicates that these needed differences are not minor variations in outlook but, at times, involve fundamental ways of thinking and behaving.

---

4    As we shall explain in more detail below, the relationship between organizational performance and internal organizational characteristics can lead to effective performance, but feedback of results also affects the way organizational states and processes develop. For example, in a high-performing organization, knowledge of success may create an atmosphere where differences in viewpoint are more acceptable and where conflict involves less tension. However, in this discussion, we will deal with the relationship as unidirectional—certain organizational characteristics leading to effective performance. We feel justified in doing this because from the viewpoint of managers or consultants concerned with corrective action, changing these internal organizational characteristics provides the best opportunity for ultimately improving performance. The reader should realize that awareness of the need to make changes is a result of feedback in the other direction (about past organizational performance).

## Integration

This model focuses attention not only upon the degree of differentiation necessary but also upon the integration required among organizational units. We need to be concerned with two aspects of the integration issue: which units are required to work together and how tight the requirement is for interdependence among them. But there is a strong inverse relationship between differentiation and integration. As we have suggested, when units (because of their particular tasks) are highly differentiated, it is more difficult to achieve integration among them than when the individuals in the units have similar ways of thinking and behaving. As a result, when groups in an organization need to be highly differentiated, but also require tight integration, it is necessary for the organization to develop more complicated integrating mechanisms. The *basic* organizational mechanism for achieving integration is, of course, the management hierarchy. In organizations with low differentiation, we have found that this is often sufficient to achieve the required intergroup collaboration. However, organizations faced with the requirement for both a high degree of differentiation and tight integration must develop *supplemental* integrating devices, such as individual coordinators, cross-unit teams, and even whole departments of individuals whose basic contribution is achieving integration among other groups. By using this model, then, we are able to understand not only the pattern of differentiation and integration required to deal effectively with a particular environment, but also the formal structural devices needed to achieve this pattern.

## Conflict Management Variables

This model also points to another set of variables which are important—the behavior patterns used to manage intergroup conflict. As individuals with different points of view attempt to attain unity of effort, conflicts inevitably arise. How well the organization will succeed in achieving integration, therefore, depends to a great extent upon how the individuals resolve their conflicts. Our work indicates that the pattern of behavior which leads to effective conflict resolution varies in certain respects depending upon environmental demands, and in other respects is the same *regardless* of variations in environmental demands.

Those conflict management factors which vary with environmental demands include the pattern of influence or power within and among groups. The influence within groups means the organizational level *at which influence or power resides* to make decisions leading to the resolution of conflict. If conflict is to be managed effectively, this influence must be concentrated at the point in the various group hierarchies where the *knowledge* to reach such decisions also exists. Obviously, this will vary depending upon the certainty of information in various parts of a particular environment. The required pattern of influence among groups also varies with environmental demands. The groups which have more critical knowledge about environmental conditions are the ones which need to have high influence in resolving intergroup conflict if the organization is to be effective in resolving such conflict.

The factors which lead to effective conflict-resolution under all environmental conditions are the mode of conflict resolution and the basis from which influence is derived. In organizations existing in quite different environments, we have found that effective conflict management occurs when the individuals deal openly with conflict and work the problem until they reach a resolution which is best in terms of total organizational goals. In essence, effective organizations confront internal conflicts, rather than smoothing them over or exercising raw power or influence to force one party to accept a solution.[5]

In organizations dealing effectively with conflict, we have also found that the individuals primarily involved in achieving integration, whether they be common superiors or persons in coordinating roles, need to have influence based largely upon their perceived *knowledge and competence.* They are followed not just because they have formal positional influence, but because they are seen as knowledgeable about the issues which have to be resolved.

To summarize, the differentiation and integration model provides a set of concepts which enable us to understand what characteristics an organization must have to be effective in a particular set of environmental circumstances. It directs our attention to environmental demands on the organization in terms of the degree of differentiation, the pattern and degree of integration, integrative mechanisms, and conflict-resolving behaviors. In sum, it provides a way of understanding much of what needs to happen at both the organization-and-environment and group-to-group interfaces.

5    This finding is consistent with the theory and findings of others. See especially *Managing Intergroup Conflict in Industry* (Blake, Shepard, and Mouton. Houston: Gulf Publishing Co., 1964).

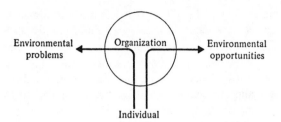

Figure 1

## SUMMARY OF THE CONCEPTUAL FRAMEWORK

We shall now summarize several points about organizations and their development that have been covered earlier in varying levels of detail. At the simplest level, we have seen that organizations start with individuals who take collective action and form an organization so that they will improve their ability to cope with their environment. In this way, the organization becomes a device for mediating between the individual and his wider environment. It provides a setting that structures and channels his transactions with the environment. It helps him engage with problems. Figure 1 symbolizes this process.

Figure 2 takes our analysis one step further. Here we see individual contributors each tied to a specific task (a dot). The individual

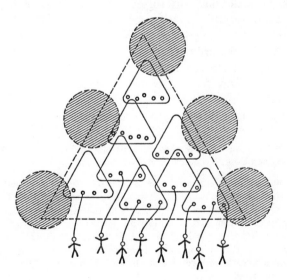

Figure 2

contributors are grouped (by the triangles) into organizational units. The environment is now depicted not as an undifferentiated mass, but as having different sectors (circles). Certain contributors are linked to these sectors to indicate their specialized task of conducting transactions with that environmental element. Each unit has developed different characteristics depending upon its part of the environment. But each unit is shown as having an integrated relationship to other units.[6] While, for simplicity, we show the integration being achieved through a shared member, we have already indicated that other mechanisms also exist to achieve integration. Finally, achieving differentiation and integration depends upon the organization members' capacity to manage conflict. In sum, this diagram depicts the basic features of our definition of organizations:

1.  the transactions between individual contributors and the organization;

2.  the pattern of differentiation of such systems as they manage the transactional strategy for dealing with the environment; and

3.  the means for achieving integration.

In Fig. 3 we take the final step in summarizing our conceptual framework by showing the key variables we have explored in a dynamic relationship to each other. This suggests the two key features of systems analysis that are stressed above—the *interdependence* of system parts, and the organization's *morphogenic* property. The variables we have placed in this model need little further explanation except to say that the rectangle denotes the organization's boundary.[7]

We see the now familiar transactional strategy as straddling the boundary with the environment. The concept of goals has been introduced simply to indicate that a strategy includes an expected target. We see that

6    This follows the "linking pin" idea developed by Likert in *The Human Organization* (New York: McGraw-Hill, 1967).

7    The boundary of an organization is particularly resistant to definition because of the fact that organizations can readily modify their own structure. For example, we would ordinarily expect to place a supplying subcontractor outside the formal legal boundary of a business organization, but his relation to the organization may become so close, so exclusive, and so interdependent that, for other purposes, it would make sense to treat the subcontractor as *inside* the boundary. The placement of organizational boundaries will continue to be a difficult issue simply because of this characteristic of organizations.

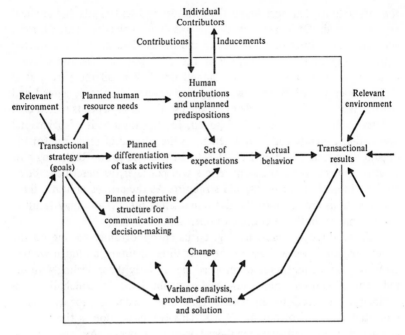

**Figure 3**

this strategy is tightly related to three internal elements: planned human-resource needs, planned differentiated task-activities, and a planned integrating structure for the necessary intergroup communication and decision-making. Planned human-resource needs are one determinant of the actual human contributions realized from working out the contribution-inducements contracts with individual contributors.

As these contributions actually occur, we must recognize that they consist of not only planned-for skills and talents but also unplanned characteristics of the whole person who appears at work with all of his built-in predispositions. The total mix of planned and unplanned human needs, differentiated activities, and integrating structures and procedures combine to create a complex set of expectations among organizational contributors. Individual members come to expect of themselves and others certain specified activities, interactions, and even certain sentiments and attitudes. These include expectations about certain informal groupings of people that were not planned in the differentiated task activities.

It is this complex set of expectations that directly condition and guide the actual overt behavior of people—the actual activities performed, the interactions that occur, and the attitudes and sentiments that are held and expressed. Of course, it is this resultant behavior that, *in toto*, generates the results or outcomes in the transactions actually conducted with the environment on behalf of the organization. Was the delivery actually made according to the planned time? Were all the parts put in their proper place? Were new supplier contracts discussed, agreed and signed? Were collections made as planned so that cash deposits match cash disbursements as planned? And so on, for the thousands of behavioral events that generate (or do not generate) the surplus of resources for the organization that are essential if it is to survive and grow. Reviewing how results compare with goals, members will consider, as described above, changes in goals, procedures, and structure. As the arrows indicate, these considerations are fed into the decision-making process and may result in certain changes in the next cycle of operations.

These three diagrams have given us an opportunity to line up the conceptual tools we will use in the next three chapters, although we will elaborate these concepts as we proceed, particularly those dealing with the inducement contract and individual contributions. In concluding this summary, we need to emphasize again the feedback process that is indicated on the bottom of Fig. 3. This feedback loop is the way we characterize the organizational-development process. As organization members get information about the results of their activities measured against the organization's plans and goals, they may make changes and adjustments at any or all of the interfaces we have discussed. If they make the "right" choices, they will enable the organization to develop.

Earlier we raised the question of how one determines whether such changes from a present organizational state to a new organizational state were in the "right" or desirable direction. We now are ready to answer this question.


## DETERMINING THE DIRECTION
## FOR ORGANIZATIONAL DEVELOPMENT


Stated most simply, the criteria we use for determining whether a particular change will lead to the development of the organization at any one or all of these interfaces is whether the change will lead to either a better fit between the organization and the demands of its environment and/or to a better fit between the organization and the needs of individual contributors. For example, at the organization-environment interface, if a particular change enables specific units to conduct transactions with their part of the environment more effectively, it is in the direction of developing the organization. Similarly, if a change facilitates achieving the integration among units required in a particular environment without sacrificing differentiation, it will develop the organization at the group-to-group interface. If a particular change results in individuals being more highly motivated to contribute to organizational purposes, it is also in the direction of organization development at the individual-organization interface.

To understand, in general, how one can utilize the concepts we have discussed to determine in what specific direction change is required, let us briefly describe how we made such determinations in our own consulting activities.

1. We use the behavioral science tools and concepts described in this book to make an analysis of the environmental or task demands facing the organization and/or to analyze the needs of the particular individual contributors with whom we are concerned. From these sorts of analyses we can make a *normative prescription* as to what organizational characteristics would provide the best fit with task requirements and individual needs.

2. These tools can be used to make a *descriptive diagnosis* of the current state of the organization. How differentiated is the organization? Where are problems occurring in achieving integration? How are members managing conflict? What are the sources of individual satisfaction and dissatisfaction? Where do members feel the individual contribution contract is inadequate, etc.? This description of the organization's state along with the normative prescription can then be utilized to determine the desired direction for change.

In essence, the *diagnosis* provides a snapshot of where the organization is currently, while the *prescriptive analysis* sets the targets for change. By using these concepts in this manner, we attempt to determine in any particular situation the directions for change which will develop the organization to fit the needs of its members and the demands of its environment.

## STAGES OF ORGANIZATION DEVELOPMENT WORK

In essence, what we have described above is the way we use these concepts in the first stage of organizational-development work, *diagnosis*. As we suggested above, this diagnostic stage is usually triggered by the awareness of some discrepancy between expected and desired outcome (goals) and actual results. We usually think of this as a way of spotting trouble when the results are on the low side. However, it is just as much a way of locating *unanticipated opportunities* when results are on the high side. In any event, it is simply a trigger. The discrepancy does not explain and account for itself. A trouble must be converted into a defined problem amenable to understanding by the process of collecting and analyzing data for causal factors.

Relevant data may be collected on any of the variables we have identified in our model, including, of course, changes in the environment. Collecting data means not only assembling quantitative evidence through questionnaires and by other means, but also talking with concerned people. The variance is bound to have multiple causes. Some of the causes will have such weak impact that they can be safely ignored—and others will have an impact that must not be ignored if the diagnosis is to be useful. For our diagnostic work we attempt to identify the multiple causes of the problem and their interrelationship. We also attempt to establish which system variables are most importantly contributing to the problem.

However, the diagnostic phase is only one of the several stages that we conceive of in organizational-development work. The others are action planning, implementation, and evaluation. We now want to review each of these in the order in which they usually occur. As we do so, two facts should be recognized:

1.  While we treat them as separate stages, in practice they are highly overlapping and interconnected. This fact will become apparent in the subsequent chapters.

2.  The concepts which we have described above also are useful in planning and carrying out these later stages. This, too, will be dealt with in detail in the subsequent chapters.

Several questions must be addressed in the *action-planning* phase, which is the second stage of organization-development work. Who are the people who are motivated to make a change attempt? What are their points of influence and leverage on the system? What variables can they most readily affect? The answers to these questions can guide a search for several alternative plans of action which show promise of altering the performance of the system in the desired direction. Action interventions can be of several types:

a)   of an educational nature—that is, they are designed to change the expectations of contributors;

b)    of a structural nature—that is, a modification of division of labor, of the planned communication network, of the contribution-inducement contract, etc.; or

c)    a change in the basic transactional strategy of the organization.

Either a strategic or a structural change usually requires an educational follow-up before the planned change can be eventually reflected in changed behavior. When several alternative action plans are available, they can be weighed against one another and the one that offers the best hope for success can then be selected for implementation.

The third phase, action *implementation*, translates the selected plan into actual behavior. The implementation will usually need to follow a phased time sequence. Intermittent checks can be made on the planned progress. This starts the final phase of *evaluation*, which is both the last step in the organizational-development sequence and the first phase of a new cycle. It consists, again, of comparing planned goals with actual results and diagnosing the variance and its causes. At this point, there is a hazard that the change goals could be treated as an end in themselves instead of a means of addressing the original discrepancy between strategic goals and results. When this occurs, it indicates that the persons involved in the development program have allowed the feedback loop to become closed, and at this point, organizational development will stop. This is a danger against which the approach emphasized in this book attempts to guard.

## PROBLEMS, CONCEPTS, AND CHANGE

In the balance of this book, we will describe in more detail our approach to organization development. As we do so, we will be dealing with three central themes. First, we will be considering the problems of organization development which exist at each of the three interfaces. Second, we will be elaborating on the concepts we have discussed and will describe how we use these tools to attack organization-development problems at each interface. Third, we will consider the process of change and its relation to the stages of organization-development activity. Descriptions of actual problem situations will be utilized to clarify and illustrate these themes.

We will deal with the organization-and-environment interface in Chapter 3, emphasizing how we use the differentiation-and-integration model to deal with these issues, and also examining the various action alternatives which managers can consider in the action-planning stage. In

Chapter 4 we will cover the group-to-group interface, again using the differentiation-and-integration conceptual scheme. Here we will put more emphasis on how we use these tools, not only in diagnosis and action-planning but also in implementation. Chapter 5 will deal with the individual-organization interface. We shall introduce in more detail the concepts we utilize to work on issues at this interface, and shall also illustrate how they are helpful not only in diagnosis but also in planning and implementing change. The final chapter draws these three themes together and relates our approach in organization-development work to several larger societal issues.

# 3
# ORGANIZATION-ENVIRONMENT INTERFACE

It is no mystery that organizations must carry on transactions with their environment simply to survive, and, even more importantly, to grow. In the first chapter, we identified the quality of these transactions as posing one of the fundamental developmental problems of any organization. Other analysts of organizational affairs have consistently mentioned transactions with the environment as a crucial if not the most crucial issue. It is an issue that has been dealt with extensively by economists and by specialists in business policy and strategy. They have dealt primarily with the content of these relationships—the actual kind and amount of goods, services, and funds that are part of these transactions. But the issue has not been extensively studied by specialists in the application of behavioral sciences, and attention has not been focused on such human aspects affecting the quality of these transactions as: What is the quality of the information exchanged across the organizational boundaries? What are the major determinants of the quality? What are its consequences?[1] Such questions have been asked many times of the relations between individuals and groups within the organization, but the boundary-spanning relations have simply not been subjected to comparable scrutiny. It is not surprising therefore, that systematic efforts to diagnose and improve the quality of these organization-environment relations have also lagged behind the effort applied to improving internal relations. It is worth speculating about the reasons for this lack of attention.

1  One notable exception has been the work on boundary transactions reported in *Organizational Stress*, Kahn *et al.* (New York: John Wiley and Sons, 1964).

23

Perhaps the focus has been placed on internal transactions because both parties to a faulty relation, being within the institution, tend to bring their troubles to a single source—their shared superior up the chain of command. This focuses attention on the costs of unsatisfactory work relations and triggers corrective action. There is less likelihood that this will happen in connection with boundary transactions. It is, moreover, not so easy to collect information about the status of the boundary-spanning relation since the outside participants may feel no obligation to cooperate. The relative neglect may also be due to the traditional division of labor between academic disciplines. It may be automatically assumed that economists are the experts on boundary transactions while the psychologist and the sociologist are expected to confine their efforts to internal relations. Even within business schools, it is traditional for the functional specialties, such as marketing and finance, to have exclusive concern with the quality of salesman-customer and treasurer-banker relationships. Only recently have such specialists drawn on behavioral disciplines to aid them in the study of these matters.

The authors themselves became involved in the study and improvement of relations at this interface by approaching the topic through the back door. We had been concerned for some years with the quality of intergroup relations in organizations. This interest led us to the observation that major groups in industry displayed some distinctive characteristics that persisted in spite of efforts from top management toward consistency. We came to the conclusion that this persistence could be accounted for if these groups needed these characteristics to conduct favorable transactions with the segment of the firm's environment with which they were especially involved. So, in order to account for some important sources of intergroup conflict, we began to study each group's relations with its special segment of the environment. Our research findings tended strongly to confirm our theory. This, in turn, led us into a new interest not only in understanding these transactions from a behavioral standpoint, but also in helping organizations and their managers diagnose the quality of these relations and improve them.

## THE CERTAINTY-UNCERTAINTY CONTINUUM

Our research findings with specific relevance to this interface can be quickly summarized since they were generally reviewed in Chapter 2. We started our inquiry with the simple notion that the characteristics of an organizational unit would in some way need to match up with those of its segment of the environment if healthy transactional relations were to prevail. We were particularly interested in information flows across these boundaries. It seemed to us that if the sector of the environment involved was in a fairly steady, unchanging state, the amount and complexity of the information needed would be much less than if the opposite were true—namely, if there existed a high degree of uncertainty and change in the relevant part of the environment. As the environment varies along this certainty-uncertainty continuum, we expected to find matching differences in the organizational unit concerned if the transactions were to be sound. We identified four measurable features of groups that we thought might vary with the certainty-uncertainty of their parts of the environment. These were:

1.  the degree of reliance on formalized rules and formal communication channels within the unit;

2.  the time horizon of managers and professionals in the groups;

3.  their orientation toward goals, either diffuse or concentrated; and

4.  their interpersonal style, either relationship- or task-oriented.

Using measures of these four characteristics, we made a study of high- and low-performing companies in three different industries, and arrived at the specific conclusion that there was a closer fit in the high-performing organizations than in the low performers between the attributes of each unit and the demands of its relevant part of the environment.[2]

One way to visualize the meaning of these findings is to think again in terms of information flows. In order to relate effectively to its environment, any organization must have reasonably accurate and timely information about the environment and especially about environmental changes. This is clearly an easier job if the environment is relatively stable. The job can be specified in a predetermined set of operating rules. The necessary messages can be handled through the traditional superior-subordinate channels, which may be few and constricted but are probably less subject to error and relatively inexpensive. Fairly short time horizons are usually adequate to take account of the reactions of such an environment to the firm's actions. This makes it sensible to use a straightforward, task-oriented approach in managerial style.

---

2    Lawrence and Lorsch, *Op. cit.*

On the other hand, life in an organizational unit must become more complex in order to deal adequately with an uncertain and rapidly changing sector of the environment. To have more points of contact with the environment, a flatter organization is employed. Formal rules cannot be formulated that will be suitable for any appreciable time period, so it seems better not to rely heavily on them. More of an all-to-all communications pattern is indicated, which can keep environmental clues moving throughout the unit for interpretation at all points instead of just through superior-subordinate channels. A longer time orientation is usually needed. The growth of this necessarily more complex and sophisticated (as well as more costly) communication network is fostered by an interpersonal style that emphasizes building strong relationships rather than just accomplishing the task, *per se*.

## STABILITY *VS.* CHANGE IN THE ENVIRONMENT

Securing and processing relevant information from the environment, while highly critical, is not the only requirement for high-quality transactions at the organization-environment interface. In addition to exchanging information, people at these interfaces must frequently negotiate the terms of exchange of tangible goods and less tangible services of many kinds. These bargaining and/or problem-solving kinds of relationships can also be analyzed in terms of the findings of research. Fouraker has used his findings from experimental research to develop the idea that organizational units with different internal features are more or less effective depending upon whether their environment is characterized by harsh competition for scarce resources or by more beneficent circumstances.[3] In a relatively unchanging environment, it is likely that time has brought more competitors into the struggle and that therefore resources are scarce. In this circumstance, he argues that the organizations which can conduct more favorable transactions will operate with tighter internal controls, more rules, and simpler channels of communication. In short, they will have closed ranks and geared up for a competitive fight. Again, it is a matching process.

At the other extreme is an organization unit dealing with a rapidly changing environment. The resources are plentiful and diverse, but the organization must be capable of creative and flexible problem-solving to

---

3    L. E. Fouraker, unpublished manuscript.

discover potential opportunities for conducting more favorable transactions. Here again that unit will thrive which relies not on rules but on a more complex and flatter communication network which serves to stimulate new ideas. Such a unit would be oriented to a longer time perspective. It would thus be matched with the features of its environment as it works at solving the problem of defining and continually redefining the terms of its environmental transactions.

These, then, are the highlights of current research on the matching of organizational units with their respective sectors of the environment. Good matching seems to foster sound transactions at this organization-environment interface. In our research we studied this interface only for the important functions of sales, research, and production; but Fig. 4 indicates how many additional interfaces of this type are relevant to most business organizations. Similar lists could be drawn for other types of organizations.

| Organizational Unit | Relevant Environmental Sector |
|---|---|
| Sales | Customers and competitors |
| Research | Science and technology |
| Production and engineering | Technology and equipment suppliers |
| Purchasing | Suppliers |
| Finance | Financial institutions |
| Personnel | Labor and professional markets |
| Public relations | The press and legislative bodies |
| Legal | Governmental regulatory agencies |

Figure 4

One of the ways of evolving an overall strategy for any organization is to develop within the organization the capacity to carry on fully adequate transactions at each of these important interfaces, with some special advantages in regard to one or two of them where a favorable exchange is possible. These are areas of "distinctive competence," to use Selznik's term.[4] An organization in which each of its boundary-spanning units is

4    P. Selznik, *Leadership Administration* (Chicago: Row Peterson, 1957), p. 8-42.

well matched with its corresponding environmental sector is in a desirable position to detect opportunities for new kinds of favorable transactions with the environment and to anticipate newly developing hazards in the environment. This matching process is a highly flexible way to maintain the kind of continuous search that is recommended by a pioneering study recently conducted by Aguilar on how business firms scan their relevant environments.[5]

As the relevant environment changes, however, organizations not only need suitable matched units, but on occasion also need to establish new units to address newly emerging environmental facts and to regroup old units. For instance, the emergence of the computer as a new environmental fact has led many firms to create a new unit such as management-information services; and the development of newly relevant mathematical techniques has led to the emergence of operations-research groups and long-range planning groups. Such new groups not only draw together people with different technical skills, but also they often need different orientations, structures, and styles to transact their business successfully.

In addition, as firms grow in terms of product variety and geographical coverage, a need frequently arises to switch the first big structural division of work in the company from the traditional functional basis, implicit in our discussion so far, to some other basis. Valid arguments can be mustered for various choices of first-level structural division, but the soundest arguments will be based on environmental facts. For instance, if different geographical areas require quite different ways of marketing, while the products of a firm are quite similar technically, a first-level split *by geography* is usually indicated, and vice versa. If, on the other hand, the products and the geographical conditions are relatively homogeneous, an initial division *by function* is probably the soundest basis.

This analysis of differences and similarities needs to be complemented by an analysis of the intensity of the interdependencies between various units to find the best possible trade-off. Once the primary basis for structurally dividing work is selected, secondary means can be provided not only at lower levels but also by staff groups. In some instances where two factors, such as functions and products, are both highly different and critical, some firms, as in the aerospace industry, are turning to a matrix

5    F. J. Aguilar, *Scanning the Business Environment* (New York: The Macmillan Co., 1967).

organization. In such an organization two bases are used simultaneously as a first-level division of labor.

We have seen that whether we view the environmental transaction primarily as a problem of information exchange or as one of bargaining and problem-solving, we are pointed toward a matching of organizational traits and orientations with environmental features. We are now in a position to explain how we use this method of analysis as a practical tool in helping specific organizations improve the quality of their environmental transactions. We will do this by examining several specific cases.

The first set of cases involves situations where mismatches could be directly addressed by making adjustments in the internal arrangements of the unit concerned. A second set of cases will also be examined where other types of adjustments were needed to improve the matching process:

1. by releasing counterpressures in the organization for consistency among all units;

2. by adjusting units to accommodate shifts in the environment;

3. by creating new units to meet newly important environmental conditions; and

4. by realigning units to cope with the increased scope of the business.

In reviewing these cases emphasis will be given to the variety of variables in the organizational systems that were selected as the initial means of implementing planned change.

Before turning to the cases, however, we need to get a feel for the way problems at this interface are likely to first present themselves to managers and in turn to behaviorally-oriented consultants. Problems at the environment-organization interface are likely to manifest themselves eventually through economic results. For example, at the sales-customer interface, it is in a loss of sales volume; in research and development, it is in a drop in the flow of new products, etc. However, these indicators of interface trouble are fairly slow to show up, and managers learn to be sensitive to earlier clues of difficulty. These often take the form of complaints from the outside—letters from customers, a private word dropped at lunch by a banker, an important move by a competitor that caught everyone flatfooted. The customer may be saying that your organization is unresponsive, that you cannot seem to tailor your products to his needs, that he is getting tired of fighting his way through your red tape. In other cases, the concern will develop because a competitor seems too frequently to be first with a new-product introduction, or a new marketing technique. Perhaps in the production area it is a failure to realize economies through process innovation or falling behind in the race with rising wages and salaries. Another clue might be that the best specialists are not staying in the company—there is a worrisome amount of turnover among the more promising professionals in the physical or managerial sciences. These are the clues that might well be traced back to human problems at the environment-organization interface.

## EXAMPLES OF ORGANIZATION-ENVIRONMENT MISMATCHES

Our first case of an organizational development problem at this interface was initially identified by worrisome symptoms of an economic nature. During our research activity in an organization developing, marketing, and manufacturing plastics products, we heard numerous complaints that the basic research laboratory was not turning out new process and product ideas. An analysis of the data we had collected on organizational practices in this laboratory revealed that the laboratory had a highly peaked management hierarchy, with most of the decisions being made exclusively by higher management. This was clearly inconsistent with the uncertainty and complexity of the information with which these scientists were expected to deal. The scientists complained that they did not have enough autonomy to follow research leads which seemed highly important to them. As one lower-level research administrator put it:

> When one project gets killed, we get another one. This is a sore point with me because we aren't given a chance to look around ourselves for new projects. We are given a project and told to work on it. My objection is that we don't give the group leader and the bench chemist the time to investigate different problems before they are being thrust into a [management-defined] program. . . .

This high degree of formalized decision-making made it difficult for these scientists to carry on meaningful transactions with the dynamic environment confronting them. It was difficult for them to freely respond to new information from the scientific environment. In addition, they had neither the authority to make decisions about research activities nor direct access to persons with market information, which could have enabled them to make effective decisions. In addition to constraining and confusing the flow of environmental information into this unit, this inappropriate structure undoubtedly also affected the motivation of these scientists. We will develop this theme in some detail in the fifth chapter. The remedy for this sort of problem is not hard to see. Find ways of getting lower-level scientists and managers more involved in decision-making, and in general loosen up the structure. While we were involved only as researchers, and thus were not expected to propose such actions, it is interesting to note that individual laboratory members were already finding ways out of these constraints. As one research manager put it:

> The individual chemist can initiate a program to a greater degree than the research manager would like to believe. It isn't always possible to get the control [the managers want] because what's going on in a certain project is always linked somewhat to the influence of the man who is working on it.

This kind of *sub rosa* response probably improves matters to some extent, but it is suboptimal as compared with forthright mutual decision-making between junior and senior people.

A more complicated problem at the organization-environment interface is illustrated by a situation which one of the authors encountered in his consulting activities. The organization in question was a unit of a major chemical company which had as its assigned mission the development, manufacture, and marketing of entirely new and unique products which did not fall within the realm of existing product divisions. Once this division, which we shall label the New Products Division (NPD), had demonstrated that a product was commercially successful, the product was transferred to an existing division, or a new division was established for it. The NPD thus dealt with products for only a limited time and during the most uncertain phase of their existence, when both markets and technology were ill-defined. In sum, the parts of the environment confronting this organization were highly uncertain.

The NPD had sales, development, and research units and drew upon various manufacturing facilities within the company, depending upon the nature of the particular product. The division general manager was aware of what he considered to be an unhealthy amount of conflict among all of these functional units, but particularly between sales and development. As a result, he asked that we help him define the nature and causes of these conflicts and then help him develop solutions to these problems. Accordingly, a diagnostic study was undertaken.

The study confirmed that the organization was achieving relatively poor integration between the functional units, and that certain conflict-management practices were not as effective as they might be. But, central to the issues we are considering here, the diagnosis also revealed that the differentiation within the organization was not in tune with its environmental demands. While the research and the development units both had structure and member orientations that were consistent with their task requirements, the sales unit did not. Whereas members of the sales unit needed to have a relatively short-term time orientation and a strong marketing-goal orientation, they actually had a long-term time horizon and were oriented toward a balance of technical and market goals. In fact, along these two dimensions, the sales unit was almost identical to the development unit. What seemed to be happening was that the two units were trying to perform the same task, and, in essence, were competing with each other for control of this task. This competition was one important source of the poor integration and unresolved conflict about which the general manager was concerned.[6]

The reason that the sales unit had drifted into the sphere of the development group was not difficult to explain. At the time of our involvement, the NPD had not yet brought many products to the stage where an active test marketing program was required. As a result, the kind of information with which the managers in the sales unit were accustomed to dealing just did not exist. However, these managers wanted something to do so they began taking a longer-range look at potential markets. As a consequence, they were dealing with information which was the legitimate concern of developmental personnel. This threatened the position of the latter group and hostility developed between the groups, making it difficult for them to cooperate.

With this data and this explanation in hand, we made a feedback presentation to the general manager and his chief subordinates. The data and their implications were accepted without too much difficulty by the general manager, the research manager, and even the development

---

6  The reader will recognize that poor integration with low differentiation is contrary to the basic antagonism between these two states, which was described in Chapter 1. Although this is the only case of such low differentiation the authors have found and it is therefore dangerous to generalize, it does suggest that the inverse relationship between differentiation and integration may not be a straight line. Instead, it may be curvilinear, with both high and low differentiation being associated with poor integration. High differentiation leads to problems of communication between units and makes integration difficult to achieve. Extremely low differentiation means the units have begun to deal with the same parts of the environment and are basically in competition.

manager. The sales manager, however, showed a great deal of resistance to this interpretation. The chief reason for this was that accepting this interpretation brought into serious question the role of his unit in the organization for the immediate future. He had brought together a group of five experienced sales managers, and had gotten them involved in identifying market opportunities, since there was very little to be done in marketing with the few new products already available. Accepting our interpretation meant either finding a more appropriate activity for these managers, which was not possible without something to sell, or having them reassigned to another division. The latter obviously would involve a loss of face for the sales manager.

Because of this resistance from the sales manager, several sessions of this management group were held with and without the consultant present. Ultimately, even though some limited progress was made in working through this problem, the general manager concluded that the most viable solution, given the bind in which the sales manager was caught, was to have him reassigned to another job of equal status and responsibility. This was accomplished and his replacement reduced the size of the sales unit and limited its activity to dealing with more immediate market issues. As a result, much of the tension between the marketing and development groups was relieved. With each unit having orientations fitting the information requirements of its task, the organization seemed to function more effectively.

As a final brief example of a rather unusual form of mismatching at the environment-organization interface, we cite a particular unit of a large electronics manufacturing firm which was charged with doing research, development, and manufacturing of some esoteric types of semiconductors. It put a heavy emphasis on participatory management, with an extensive use of product teams for decision purposes. There was also careful planning of physical arrangements so as to facilitate necessary interactions between groups. Management officials hoped to secure high involvement from all levels and a working climate that induced creative work. In many ways their experiment succeeded, but they were troubled by serious complaints from many of the specialized engineering and technical people who held critical positions. The comments below from some of these people indicate the nature of their concerns:

> In a way, the [unit] is not a satisfying place for the [technical] professional. You seem to have to go through a lot of red tape and coordination to get something technical done.

The technical guy is principally interested in technical things and the business team in economic problems. There's a certain type of research-oriented person who would be completely frustrated in the team. He's not interested in business or human relations unless they have a direct bearing on what he's doing.

I'm basically a scientist. Scientists are individualists and you appreciate freedom in your thoughts and action. And this basically goes across the grain of the business team.

The complaints stand in sharp contrast to the highly favorable responses of almost all of the nontechnical personnel. This contrast became apparent to one of the authors in the course of research in preparing a teaching case. The senior officials of the unit, upon seeing the pattern, concluded that the heavy emphasis being placed on securing integration through the use of group methods had not allowed the technical people enough of an opportunity to differentiate their role and orientation. A careful internal study was made of the issue, and a modification of the group procedures was adopted. This seemed to correct the situation. In essence, the engineering personnel were freed from involvement in business activity, and an integrator was provided to link them to these activities. Thus technical personnel were freer to develop orientations related to their major task.

## OTHER VARIETIES OF
## ORGANIZATION-ENVIRONMENT PROBLEMS

Not all of the issues involving transactions between the environment and organizational units appear as the kind of mismatch situations that can be directly addressed in the manner we have been reviewing. The examples presented below indicate the range and variety of other problems that can now be more systematically analyzed at this interface and moved through the entire development cycle on a more predictable basis.

The first example involves the relation between headquarters and field units and the impact these had on environmental transactions. One of the authors had the opportunity to take part in the efforts of a large "heavy industry" firm to make adjustments in their geographically dispersed production units that would improve the match with their respective environments. This issue had been addressed under a number of different headings in this company and in a number of ways, but the key issue had remained the same. At one time or another, it had been called a line-staff problem, a headquarters-field problem, and a centralization-*vs.*-decentralization problem. In a variety of ways, the company had been working repeatedly through the diagnosis, planning, action, and evaluation cycle of change. The trend over several years had been away from an earlier insistence on company-wide consistency and toward greater local autonomy in order to foster better matching with environmental conditions. It is revealing to review the history of these change efforts and, in particular, a recent major educational intervention.

This company had gone through an earlier period of rapid expansion as it exploited an advantage it enjoyed in securing one of its basic raw materials at a significantly lower cost than its competitors. During this period, it was not crucial that each and every one of its major plants be optimally matched with its respective local environmental conditions. But as the company gradually lost its original unique advantage, these matching issues became important. However, a tradition had become well established that the various aspects of the business were largely controlled from headquarters, with each central functional department dominating its respective affairs throughout the organization. For instance, the central engineering group had the dominant voice not only in new construction but also in new-equipment decisions and production-process modifications. The same largely held for other functions such as accounting, purchasing, quality-control, transportation, and personnel. This affected a set of widely scattered plants that roughly did one of two types of work—basic bulk manufacturing or secondary fabrication work. The managers in these outlying locations began to perceive that many opportunities for performance improvement in their local environments were being lost because of the demand for consistency from the center.

With this issue as one of its principal objectives, the company decided to undertake an extensive educational program. A considerable number of managers were sponsored in attending sensitivity-training sessions. This was later followed up by conducting "family" work-planning conferences of three or four days' duration for members of a managerial group. A few laboratory-training sessions were organized on an intergroup basis that brought together such pairs of groups as managers at headquarters from some one function with managers from a major plant concerned with the same functional specialty. At about this time, the company decided to make a formal structural separation of the management of the basic material plants from the management of the fabricating units. A major reason for the decision was that the fabricating plants were in need of a shorter-term and more market-oriented management in contrast to the longer-term and cost-oriented management customary in the basic plants. The structural step was designed to foster the needed differentiation, but it was initially not well understood by middle management.

At this point, one of the authors became involved in the further planning and implementing of this company's push toward fitting its units with environmental requisites. A small planning group of senior company managers and outside consultants undertook to further diagnose the company situation. In spite of progress being made by earlier change efforts, this top group was not satisfied with the quality of the intergroup relations and the responsiveness of major units to changes in the environment. When this planning group found they were in agreement in their size-up of the situation, they decided to proceed with a major additional educational effort rather than undertaking a more systematic diagnostic study. Plans were developed for bringing together the general managers of all the major plants and the heads of all the headquarters departments in a training design that called for three one-week sessions spaced three to four months apart. The theme of the sessions was the managing of corporate change.

The training group, when assembled, decided to focus its efforts on assessing environmental changes and identifying shared company problems. Two issues emerged as being of paramount importance. One was the repercussions in the company of the recent structural separation of the basic and fabricating units. This change was seen as threatening the sense of overall unity in the company or what might be called "the one big family" feeling. This change needed to be assimilated on both a cognitive and an emotional basis. At the cognitive level, the participants were exposed to the logic of the move in terms of environmental demands and the concepts of differentiation and integration. The representatives of the various units then described to the total group the typical problems and issues they faced in their respective environments. Striking differences became apparent that they had not fully appreciated before.[7] As these realities were clarified, the structural split met with more emotional acceptance without the loss of mutual respect.

---

7    An associated program, conducting an exchange of plant visitations by contrasting pairs during the interval between sessions, served to reinforce these perceptions of differences and the necessity for them.

The second major issue that emerged was the relation between the headquarters departments and the basic manufacturing plants. The central departments felt under pressure to permit more of their functions to be performed under plant control. They were becoming very uncomfortable with this trend, and tended to ascribe it simply to a fad for decentralization. Meanwhile the plant people were still feeling unnecessarily constricted by the rules and regulations of at least some of the central units. Once again, these issues were directly faced both by examining in detail their specifics on a function-by-function basis and by drawing on the general concept of differentiation and integration to provide a framework for systematic thinking. The net effect of these sessions was to see:

1. the very real business need for further relaxation of some of the rules designed to enforce consistency;

2. the need for a careful sorting of functions between the center and the plants in terms of the locus of relevant skills and pertinent information; and

3. the need for more open communication channels for the continuing adjustment of mutual problems between the center and the field.

The thrust was toward greater differentiation without losing integration; and, of course, the greater differentiation was designed to further the matching of the outlying units with their changing environmental circumstances.

At the end of the third residential session, the participants undertook to do their own evaluation of the program. Some of the program values they emphasized as having been realized were: "design of work procedures for examining and defining service unit role," "construction of a cross-company network of good will, communication, and trust for future problem-solving," and "greater insight into company's overall operations and problems." In addition, they arranged to have their group act as a resource panel to work on the detailed review of the division of work between headquarters and the field plants on a function-by-function basis.

This program *in toto* can be characterized as emphasizing an educational type of intervention to improve the matching at the environmental-organizational interface. In effect, it approached the problem obliquely by releasing the constraining pressures from the headquarters departments rather than by driving directly toward the matching of environmental demands with unit characteristics. When the problem is defined as seeking a change in a field of forces, as suggested by Kurt Lewin, this emphasis on relaxing a constraining force can be fully as effective as a more direct approach. This theoretical conclusion is supported by the available facts in this instance. This case also put an emphasis on education as the major lever of change, with only a sketchy use of systematic diagnosis. Much of the diagnosis was done by drawing from the perceptions of the managers during the early part of the training sessions. This method tended to increase the sense of involvement by these men, but at some cost in the specificity of the diagnosis. It should also not be ignored that one important part of the change was the structural shift of formally splitting the basic and fabricating units. In our judgment, this formal differentiation was needed to better match the environmental requirements, but the education effort was also needed to assimilate this change.

To turn to another case, the authors have been involved over a period of several years in working with a major company in the consumer packaged-food industry, which faced a major problem in realigning itself with its market environment. This company had been highly successful in conducting a decentralized business, with geographically dispersed sales units performing the final packaging and marketing functions. The market environment had been relatively stable for more than a generation. Few changes were needed in product or marketing methods to build upon an earlier innovative period. As a result, the outlying units had evolved some highly detailed routines for handling the products.

In recent years, this market environment had become much more turbulent. New products and packages were being sought by customers. New sales outlets were coming into being. The company had, of course, been responding to these changes, but rather sluggishly, and seldom as the innovator. The field units that performed so well under stable conditions were faced with an environment where change was becoming a steady pattern rather than an occasional event. Some more fundamental changes in the units were needed to secure responses that went beyond firefighting and counterpunching.

As this diagnosis emerged, the company undertook a major and continuing educational program directed toward these decentralized units. The program has addressed various topics but with a consistent method. The method has been to expose the managers concerned to the facts of relevant environmental change around a given topic and then to push them into struggling with the implications of these changes for their own organizations. There has been a heavy reliance on the use of teaching cases as materials for discussion and analysis. Different aspects of the business were reviewed in this manner. The managers have not been told how to respond but have been helped to develop more appropriate problem-solving methods.

As this effort has proceeded, there has been a clearly noticeable change in the behavior of these managers. They consistently testify to the improvement of their general ability to tackle new problems. Their enhanced sense of competence has made them willing to search their environments more thoroughly for early signs of opportunities or threats. The speed of response of their organizations seems to have improved considerably. In short, they are on the road to learning to exist successfully in a more dynamic environment.

The final two examples involve situations where formal structural change was the key element in the change process. In the first situation the R & D units of a large petrochemical organization were diagnosed as having become so heavily development-oriented that long-term basic research was relatively neglected. The company decided to create an essentially new unit that would be carefully tailored to perform the desired research job. In this situation, the authors were asked to provide assistance in the analysis of the relevant scientific environment in order to specify roughly how the new unit should be organized to improve the probabilities of success at this organization-environment interface. This included consideration of recruitment criteria, formal structure, internal departmental procedures, physical layout, and communication linkages with other company units. It is much too early to assess results in this instance, but it is clear that the managers involved have already achieved a much clearer sense of where they are going and how they are going to get there than is the usual pattern. They have been able to obtain a higher level of agreement on the specific points of their organization plan and on its overall integrity.

In another quite different application a general manager in a consumer-goods field was being pressed by his superior to restructure his major division from a functional basis of first-order differentiation to a product basis. The manager agreed with the argument that the rapid state of proliferation of new products in his unit would eventually warrant such a reorganization. The question was, when? He felt that the recent success of his unit stemmed principally from a highly creative development group that not only worked together effectively as a total group, but had also managed to develop some fairly strong working links with both the marketing and manufacturing units. He feared that a premature reorganization would disrupt this innovative combination. A procedure was developed by which he could secure periodic readings on his organization to improve the timing of the inevitable reorganization. In effect, differentiation and integration measurements were devised to answer the following question: When would the loss of effectiveness because of the simultaneous handling of multiple products exceed the gain of keeping a close interchange going between all the development specialists? This application indicated that more substantive data can be a useful guide on this kind of complex timing issue.

## CONCLUSION

The examples cited above all present some variant of an organization-environment interface problem. Taken together, they illustrate the considerable range of practical issues that are becoming amenable to more systematic study and action, using concepts and methods adapted from the behavioral sciences. In these situations, it has not always been appropriate or possible to put equal emphasis on all phases of the change cycle. Flexibility is needed; for instance, the diagnostic phase varied from highly specific and quantified work to more qualitative studies based upon the shared observations of managers.

We should particularly note that the goals of change have been sought in these cases by using a wide variety of methods. Specifically designed educational programs have been employed that used various pedagogical techniques. Shifts in the formal structure have been employed ranging from major reorganization to shifts in the content of particular roles and their incumbents. The wide range of variables used might suggest a more chaotic rather than a more systematic approach to improvement of organization-environment transactions if it were not for a consistent set of concepts and diagnostic methods that were applied in each case. Clarity of conceptualization has fostered flexibility in the choice of change methods.

The use of behavioral methods to seek improvement in the fit between organizational units and their sectors of the environment is a relatively new field of application. The early steps in this direction which the authors report here are suggestive of a much wider array of possible future applications.

# 4

# THE GROUP-TO-GROUP INTERFACE

As we have already indicated, if organizations are to deal effectively with their environment they have to be differentiated into groups of individual contributors, each of which manages the transactions with a part of the organization's total environment. The second set of organizational development issues, maintaining and improving relationships at the interfaces among these groups, emerges as a result of this differentiation among organizational units. The objective of organizational development efforts at this interface is to achieve collaboration or integration between these groups of specialized contributors so that they can make a coordinated effort toward total organizational goals, while still working effectively at managing the transactions with their particular segment of the environment.

## PRESENTING ISSUES AT THIS INTERFACE

Managers who come to us seeking help in improving the functioning of their organization at this interface complain about a variety of symptoms, but they usually have difficulty identifying the source of the problem. For example, they express concern because the expectations of participants on each side of an interface have developed in such a way that they are playing a win-lose game with each other. They see each group stoutly defending its own position with the belief that to do otherwise would

41

result in a defeat of some sort. Similarly, managers may state their view of the problem in this way:

> Important decisions are dropping between the chairs. Each group thinks the other is handling a problem and as a result no one deals with it.

Managers who have this concern often attribute the difficulty to a "communication breakdown."

> The groups which need to work together just aren't communicating. We need help in getting them to talk to each other.

When the issues raised by managers are at this level of concreteness, we feel fortunate. At least they have recognized that there is a problem at the interface between two or more groups or units. This is a big help, even though we and they may later learn that their description of the behavioral symptoms and their causes is misleading and inaccurate.

However, more often than not we find that managers are unable to be specific in defining problems. More frequently, they may have become aware, as a result of feedback from the environment, that their competition is operating more effectively than they. Perhaps they discover that competitors are turning out more or better new products, or that competition is providing better customer delivery and service. Typically the managers have considered possible technical and economic causes for their problem and have concluded that these are not at the root of the matter. A vague sense of uneasiness develops: something is wrong in the way the organization is functioning. But the managers have no clear idea of where to look for the causes of the problem or what to do about them. So they come looking for "experts" in organizational and "people" problems. When we are approached in this manner, our first step is to arrange to make a diagnosis of the nature of the underlying problems existing at this interface, so that we can move beyond these presenting symptoms. As we indicated earlier, we use the differentiation and integration model for this purpose.

### Applying Differentiation and Integration
### at the Group-to-Group Interface

Having briefly sketched out this conceptual model in the earlier chapters, we should now flesh out these short descriptions by looking at two contrasting situations in which managers were attempting to develop this interface. In so doing we shall concentrate on the use of this model as a planning tool in the diagnostic stage to identify the characteristics which an organization needs to deal effectively with its particular set of environmental issues. Later we shall pinpoint the usefulness of these tools in action planning, implementation, and evaluation.

The first organization was a business enterprise involved in developing, producing, and manufacturing basic plastic materials. We were engaged as consultants to this organization to help determine why it had not been more successful in dealing with the critical environmental issue of developing innovative products and processes.

Using the differentiation and integration model, we identified the critical environmental characteristics facing the organization. The scientific part of the environment was highly uncertain and tumultuous. New knowledge was being developed at a rapid rate. There was still high uncertainty about cause-and-effect relationships affecting the characteristics of these plastic materials. Feedback about the results of scientific work was infrequent, often occurring only after several years of work. Relevant data on the market environment were more easily obtained than in the scientific sector. Feedback about action taken was more rapid, but there was some uncertainty about competitive developments and customer requirements. Knowledge was even more certain in the techno-economic sector of the environment. The process hardware itself provided a high degree of certainty about what could and couldn't be done. Feedback of results of action taken in this sphere was very rapid, often on an hourly or at most a daily basis.

Given this variation in the degree of certainty in these three parts of the organization environment, the differentiation between the specialized groups needed to be quite high. For example, the scientific contributors needed to work in a unit which had very little formal structure. These researchers also needed to be directed toward goals of scientific discovery and to have long time horizons. In contrast the production specialists needed to be more short-term oriented and to be concerned with operating efficiencies, costs, and deliveries. Given the high certainty of their task, these specialists should work in a more formalized structure with a number of authority levels, formal rules and procedures, and specific and frequent review of individual and group performance. The sales group needed to fall between these other groups on the dimensions of structure, time, and goal orientation, but was required to be quite different from each of them in interpersonal orientation. Whereas the individuals in research and manufacturing needed to be more task-oriented to deal with their respective tasks of high and low certainty, the sales personnel needed to be more socially oriented to deal with their moderately certain task and to maintain relationships with the customer.[1]

All of this adds up to the requirement that the organization be highly differentiated. But this organization also had to achieve tight integration if it was to be successful in process and product innovation. Critical interdependence around this issue was required between the research and sales groups and between the research and production groups.

Application of these concepts also indicated that this organization would need a complicated set of integrating devices. The management hierarchy alone could not bridge the gap over these wide differences and achieve the integration required. The organization, therefore, would need to have smoothly functioning integrating roles and/or cross-functional teams.

Finally, the model pointed to the requirement for a number of conflict-management practices. First, confrontation would have to be the dominant way of resolving conflicts. While this is important in any environment, it would be particularly crucial for this organization, given the requirement for both wide differences in outlook and tight integration. Similarly, the individuals in integrating roles would need to derive their influence from their competence and knowledge if they were to be effective in helping to resolve conflicts. Another requirement for this organization, suggested by this model, which we did not mention earlier, is that individuals in the integrating roles need an outlook which is balanced between that of the specialist-contributors. If they have this balanced or intermediate viewpoint, they will be more effective in communicating with the various specialists.

With respect to the pattern of influence required to resolve conflict effectively in this organization, we need to examine influence among groups and within groups. The group of integrating personnel needed to have the highest influence (as suggested earlier it was important that this be based on their professional competence), because these individuals, with their balanced viewpoints and their knowledge, are in a crucial position to resolve conflicts along the interfaces between the functional groups. Within each group the level which was required to have the highest influence varied. In the production unit, with a highly certain task

1    This difference was suggested by the work of Fred E. Fiedler, *Technical Report No. 10*, Group Effectiveness Laboratory, Dept. of Psychology, Univ. of Illinois, May, 1962.

environment, this level had to be well up in the authority hierarchy. In the sales group, with a moderately uncertain portion of the environment, the level where influence was concentrated had to be at the middle level. Having a highly uncertain task, the research group needed influence for reaching decisions at a relatively low organizational level.

Given the demands of this particular organization's environment, we have thus outlined the characteristics needed at the group-to-group interface to conduct successful transactions with the environment and to obtain intergroup collaboration. These prescriptions can be taken as a set of targets for the managers as they plan their organizational-development strategy. Before examining how we also use these tools to obtain a description of the actual state of relations at this interface, we want to examine a contrasting situation where the environmental demands on the organization were quite different. This should provide us with a fuller understanding of the systemic or contingency nature of the differentiation-and-integration model.

In the case of the plastics business just mentioned, we were engaged as consultants and thus were involved from the initial phases of the organizational-development effort. Our involvement in the second organization which we wish to use as an example was somewhat more limited. We came upon it as part of a program of developing case material for teaching purposes. The top managers had already sought considerable consulting help, but were still confused as to what the ideal future state of their organization should be. The concepts we have been discussing proved useful to them in sorting out this issue.

This organization was a division of a major manufacturer of paper and paper products.[2] The division in question manufactured and marketed corrugated containers for a variety of industrial and commercial users. Its operations, which were on a national scale, were carried out by approximately 25 local manufacturing plants and a territorial sales organization which was aligned to correspond to these manufacturing sites. The major issue at the group-to-group interface, with which these managers were concerned, was how to achieve integration between the sales and manufacturing groups.

In attempting to determine what organizational characteristics were demanded by this organization's environment, we also started by examining the certainty of the parts of the environment. In this case we

2    Rockford Containers A, B, and C. (Copyright by the President and Fellows of Harvard College, 1967.)

concerned ourselves with only two major segments of the environment (the techno-economic and the market), since the development of new scientific knowledge was not a major issue.

For the division as a whole the market environment was relatively uncertain. It was made up of a number of local markets with quite different characteristics (e.g., the market for poultry boxes in the south central region, the citrus fruit market in California, the market for beer cases in Milwaukee). To bring some certainty into this situation, these individual markets had to be dealt with at the local level. (The requirement for local marketing and manufacturing was also reinforced by the relatively high transportation cost of the boxes.) Each local market, however, was in itself moderately uncertain. Competitive reaction to price changes was not always predictable, nor was the quantity or type of product required by customers.

The techno-economic portion of the environment was somewhat more certain. The technology itself was very stable and relatively simple. The price of raw materials was controlled by corporate headquarters, since the division's principal supplier was the parent company's paper mills. In fact the real uncertainty in this part of the environment was fed in from the market-delivery schedules, quantity, and product mix.

The required differentiation between the sales and production groups, therefore, was not great. While the sales group would require a somewhat less formalized structure than the manufacturing group and a more social interpersonal orientation, the required time and goal orientations for the two groups were quite similar. Both groups needed to be concerned with short-term almost day-to-day issues. While the production group should focus on cost efficiency and the sales group on pricing, both also needed to be concerned with goals related to the critical competitive issue of meeting customer demands for prompt delivery at the lowest possible cost.

These common goals are also closely connected to the integration required in this environment. Tight integration between the sales and production units at the local level was essential. These two groups had to jointly resolve conflicts around the constant trade-offs between customer delivery and operational efficiency, and between competitive prices and operating costs. This meant that conflict resolution was required at the local level. Since this is where the knowledge about these issues rested, decision-making influence had to be concentrated here. Similarly, both the sales and manufacturing groups had critical information about these issues and both would need to have approximately equal influence over these choices.

In sum, these environmental characteristics seemed to require an organization with relatively low differentiation between sales and manufacturing groups but with tight interdependence between these groups. The resolution of conflict between the groups had to be conducted at the local management level with balanced influence between the groups. Obviously, the model would also suggest that managers should rely on confrontation of conflict to resolve these issues. Given the relatively low differentiation, a relatively simple integrative mechanism would be suited to this organization. For example, the management hierarchy might be sufficient. Also, given the requirement for a shared goal-orientation of the two groups, the rewards and information system should emphasize superordinate goals at the local level (i.e., local profits).

While we were not engaged as consultants by these managers, we did discuss this analysis with them, and they found it useful in thinking about the objectives of their organizational-development program. However, all of us were aware of another feature of this organization which necessitated some compromise with the prescription suggested by this analysis. This division of the company had been built over the prior five years through the acquisition of twenty local independent container manufacturers. When these firms were acquired, the former owners often chose to retire or to leave the business, in order to manage their personal capital. As a consequence the organization was faced with a critical shortage of local general-management talent who could fill an integrating role at the critical local level. While our normative application of the differentiation-and-integration model suggested that the required integration could be achieved through the management hierarchy, by having a local general manager to coordinate the local plant and sales territory, the dearth of human resources in the organization made this impractical. As a result, we suggested that the manager develop management teams at the local level consisting of sales and manufacturing managers. At the regional level (each region would encompass five or six local plants and sales territories), a general manager's role would be utilized. The principal job of these regional general managers would be to develop the local management teams, particularly building skill in resolving conflicts and reaching joint decisions.

These are the organizational objectives toward which this division management is now committed. We do not wish to elaborate here on the problems of achieving these objectives. Rather we simply wish to point out that this is another example of how these concepts can be used to crystallize the objectives of an organizational-development program. It is a particularly interesting example, because it also points to the necessity of continually considering not only the environmental demands facing the organization but also the skills and needs of the individual contributors who are available to the organization.

The two examples together illustrate an important facet of our approach to organizational development at this interface. We start with the basic premise that there is no one ideal way of developing organizations at this interface. Instead, those involved in an organization-development effort must work toward their objectives while recognizing that behavior in the organization will be the result of a system of variables, including the predispositions of the individual contributors and the demands of the environment with which they are dealing.

A comparison of these two examples indicates that organizational-development objectives in these two organizations were quite different. In the corrugated container organization they were to develop a relatively simple integrating mechanism which would help members to bridge a narrow gap in outlook between two groups. In the plastics organization the differences to be bridged were much wider and the interdependencies more complex, and more complicated integrative mechanisms would be required. Not only do these two situations require different structural changes, but they also suggest somewhat different educational interventions. In the container organization, the educational effort would have to be focused on the regional managers to help them develop the skill to build local management teams. For the plastics firm a broader-based educational effort, which we will describe in detail below, was required.

We have so far illustrated how this particular set of concepts can be used to identify the ultimate goals of an organizational-development program. But earlier we mentioned that this is only one phase of the organizational-development process. One must have such a normative end in sight, but it is also necessary to have a description of the current organizational state, so that the organizational-development effort can be planned to move the organization from where it is to where the managers want it to be. We next turn to the way we use this differentiation-and-integration model to obtain a description of the organization and then to develop an educational intervention approach which motivates the managers involved to develop their organization toward the desired objectives.

## THE ORGANIZATION-DEVELOPMENT PROCESS
## AT THE GROUP-TO-GROUP INTERFACE

To understand our approach to organizational development, it may be helpful to review the stages of organizational-development work mentioned earlier: Diagnosis, Design, Action-Planning, Implementation, and Evaluation. These stages, as we indicated, are usually not sequential or discrete, but rather are intertwined. Nevertheless, bearing them in mind provides a guide to what we seek to accomplish in organizational-development work at this interface.

As already mentioned, whenever we are engaged to do organizational development work, we try to make it an explicit condition of the relationship, that the first stage will be a diagnostic study. There are two reasons for doing this, suggested by the preceding discussion: First, we want to make the type of thorough analysis of the environmental requirements (impinging on the organization at this or any interface) which we have just described. Second, we want to know as much as possible about how well the organization currently measures up to these requirements. This basic analysis is essential since, as has been suggested, most managers have only a vague notion of the problems confronting them and their causes.

These diagnostic steps, then, provide us as consultants with an understanding of the direction and scope of the changes that are required. But these diagnostic steps also have an important bearing upon designing and implementing the organizational-development effort. They provide the top managers, with whom we are working, a view of the problems around which they can develop a set of shared expectations about the necessity for and the direction of change. This can guide us and them in discussing changes in the structure of the organization and in designing the implementation effort for the rest of the organization. We will have more to say about this as we explore our approach in detail. To do this we want to return to the case of the plastics organization mentioned above. Our approach in this organization was typical of what we have tried to accomplish at this interface in a number of organizations and provides a good example.

Our first step in this organization was to make a diagnostic study of both the environmental demands and the actual situation in this organization. Information about environmental requirements was obtained through interviews with knowledgeable managers in the organization and from our own prior experience in doing research studies in other organizations in the same industry. To obtain data about the current state of the organization, we used interviews and questionnaires[3] which were designed to obtain information consistent with the differentiation-and-integration framework; that is, data about the states of differentiation and integration and the process of conflict management which existed in the organization. These data-gathering methods provided us with both clinical and quantitative data about the current internal situation in the organization. While in other situations we have used only interviews or group-interviewing techniques, we feel that the combination of quantitative and clinical data is more desirable. The quantitative data enabled us to make a systematic comparison of the current state of this organization with other organizations in a similar business and against the "ideal" desired state. The clinical data provide supporting evidence in the managers' own words for the quantitative data. This is important in establishing the credibility of the diagnostic phase. As we shall see, both of these factors contributed to the success of the implementation steps in our effort.

From the data we had collected, we gained several important insights as to the degree to which this particular organization met the requirements for dealing effectively with its environment. On the positive side we found that the various specialist groups (sales, research, and manufacturing) were appropriately differentiated to carry out transactions with their part of the environment. Each of these groups had a structure consistent with the certainty of its task, and the individuals in each group had developed orientations matching those required for the task. The reader will recall that these groups were thus highly differentiated.

Along with this strength, a number of organizational difficulties were identified, which together seemed to account for the present problem: difficulties in achieving product and process innovations. First, we found that there were a number of serious difficulties in achieving integration among the groups involved. Particularly problematic were the relationships between the applied and fundamental research groups and between these groups and the sales group. An integrating group which also did development work existed in this organization. Instead of achieving close collaboration with the sales and research groups (which had been management's aim in establishing it), the integrating group had serious integration difficulties with these other units.

3    P. R. Lawrence and J. W. Lorsch, *Organization and Environment: Managing Differentiation and Integration,* Division of Research, Harvard Business School, Boston, 1967. (See especially the "Methodology Appendix," pp. 247-268.)

Closely related to these integration problems were a number of difficulties in the manner in which conflict was handled. First, we found that while the members of the integrating department had higher influence than members of the other groups (as they should), this influence was not based primarily on their perceived competence and knowledge; instead, it seemed to derive largely from their position and their control of a number of scarce resources. This meant that members of the other groups often saw the integrators' efforts in taking the lead to resolve conflict as illegitimate and arbitrary. Related to this, we found that the members of the integrating groups did not have the balanced set of orientations which was necessary for them to be effective. Instead of balancing long- and short-range concerns, and market, research, and techno-economic concerns, they were highly oriented toward short-run market problems. This also contributed to their inability to work effectively in resolving conflict. A third problem in the conflict-management area pertained to all organization members. They reported that they were doing less confronting and more smoothing of conflict than seemed desirable.

All of these issues we identified largely through the quantitative measures developed from the questionnaire, although they were all corroborated by the interview data. Another related issue was identified exclusively from the interviews: This organization had established, in addition to the integrating department, a number of cross-functional teams as integrating mechanisms. These teams had been established at three separate levels of the organization. From interviewing the organization members, we learned that there were no clear expectations about what each level of these teams was supposed to do to achieve integration. Members of the teams were confused about what was expected of them and about how the teams were intended to accomplish better integration. Thus, we had developed a description of the organization which indicated that appropriate integrating devices existed but that they were not effective in achieving integration because of ineffective conflict-management practices and confusion about the roles of various teams.

With this information in hand, we arranged a feedback session with the general manager and the four top functional managers. Although a full day and evening session was devoted to this, the initial data presentation, which was organized around the differentiation-and-integration framework, required only a few hours. The balance of the time was spent discussing the data and working through their implications. To emphasize the relationship between these organizational factors and economic performance, we presented comparative organizational data for a highly effective organization, in the same parent corporation and in the same industry which we had studied, whose states and processes met the environmental demands almost perfectly. Our client firm's managers were familiar with the operation of the other organization and knew of its enviable economic performance. As a result they were able to accept more easily the connection between organizational factors and economic performance. This provided them with one strong incentive to admit the need for change. It also provided a clear model of the goals to aim for in their organizational-development effort.

While we were in the fortunate position of having this comparative data, such data is obviously not always available. Nevertheless, even without this type of data, the type of analysis described above, determining what an organization needs to do to manage the uncertainty in its environment, provides both a target for organizational change and an understanding of the need for the change. We have done this on several occasions and accomplished much the same result as we did here with the comparative data—an understanding of the need for organizational improvement and what improvement would entail.

It would be misleading to suggest, however, even in the example we are discussing, that the top managers all accepted immediately and without reservation the need for and direction of organizational change. There were over eight hours of discussion with us on the validity and meaning of the data presented. Subsequently, the managers discussed these same issues with each other. But by the end of the first day's session, these managers had made several important steps toward development of their organization at the group-to-group interface. First they had become familiar with and accepted to a great extent our conceptual framework for thinking about these problems. Second, they had begun to develop among themselves a set of shared expectations that organizational improvement was possible and necessary. And they developed the beginnings of a consensus about the direction such change should take. Specifically, by the end of the first session this group of five managers was committed to devoting time from their already busy schedules to organizational development. They also decided on the format of a second feedback session with their key subordinates.

As part of this second session we suggested a simulation exercise which was designed to give the participants a "here and now" exposure to dealing with conflict. While part of the first session had been devoted to examining the interpersonal processes these five managers used to resolve conflict, the organizational issues facing them were so gripping that these managers found it difficult to examine their own process. With a larger group of sixteen managers planned for the second session, we felt this type of "processing" would be even more difficult. Yet given the fact that these managers were not confronting conflict, we wanted to use these sessions to encourage more confronting behavior. We, therefore, proposed this simulation exercise. Since it was a business game involving the selection of new research and development projects, it was a particularly appropriate exercise for this group.

We kicked off the second session, which began at noon on one day and went through a full second day, by presenting the comparative data from our diagnostic study. A discussion of the meaning of the data and its implications ensued. During this phase of the meeting the top managers, who were at the first session, became actively involved in supporting the results of the study and in clarifying the meaning of the data. To us, this indicated that they were beginning to feel that they "owned" the data and had some responsibility for seeing that action to improve the organization at this interface was taken. Following this discussion of the diagnostic study on the first half day and evening, the second day was devoted to the simulation and a discussion of how that experience related to the study data.

Perhaps the most important result of this session was that the top two echelons of management had come to understand the data and were to some degree committed to planning action steps to remedy their organizational problems. Specifically, they made several decisions. First, they asked that the data be presented to all the other organization members. Along with this we agreed to develop a training intervention which would demonstrate to other organization members how their different viewpoints created integration problems. Second, as a result of the simulation exercise they realized that they had no clearly understood set of criteria to use for reaching decisions on research and development expenditures. This made it extremely difficult to confront conflicts around these important issues, since various parties to a dispute were playing the decision-making game with different sets of rules. To rectify this difficulty, they arranged for skill training for the group in economic analysis and subsequently developed a new procedure for reviewing and evaluating research and development proposals.

Two subsequent feedback sessions were held for other organization members. Each of these sessions, which lasted a day and a half, had in attendance representatives from all the functional groups. Again, we presented the data and provided time for discussion of it. After this we introduced an educational intervention which we labelled a "Differentiation Laboratory" because its purpose was to help the participants understand and appreciate the differences in their outlook. The design of this laboratory consisted of dividing the participants into groups of four—one representative from each functional group. Members of each functional group were asked to talk about what was important in accomplishing their job and what satisfaction they derived from their work. They also were asked to discuss what other functional groups did to block accomplishing their objectives. When these subgroups reconvened into a general session, a lively discussion developed in which the participants worked problems between functional groups and developed a clearer understanding of their misperceptions and stereotypes of each other and how these inhibited communication and conflict resolution.

These four sessions, in essence, represented the action planning and implementation phases of this organizational-development effort. These two phases completely overlapped. We initially designed feedback and training interventions for top management and applied them. As a result, we and these managers designed the other educational interventions described. The managers, on their own, took other action steps. We became aware of the extent to which the managers had actually gone to work on these problems about a year after the last of these feedback sessions. At this time, it seemed useful to make an appraisal of what had and had not been accomplished as a result of this program. The management of the organization readily agreed and a colleague of ours, who had not been involved in the program, interviewed members of the organization.

The managers and scientists were generally enthusiastic about what the program had accomplished. They reported that as a result of the program they had developed a more concerted effort to coordinate all of their research activity. More top management time was consciously being devoted to this activity. They were also using a new set of decision criteria to evaluate research and development projects. This was a direct result of this effort and according to them had facilitated the resolution of conflict. As a result, they felt they were doing a more effective job of planning new product innovations. Members of the cross-functional teams which were conducting this effort reported that the program had stimulated a series of discussions within and among teams about their role. They now saw more clearly the role of the various teams and how they all could contribute to their objectives. Finally, the members of the integrating group indicated they were devoting more time to working with other functional groups, enabling research to get a unified new product effort. According to organization members, all of this added up to improved organizational integration without sacrificing differentiation.

The reader may wonder how a diagnostic study and four relatively short feedback discussions could accomplish so much. The answer to this can best be understood by reviewing at a more general level what managers report they have gained from this approach to organizational development. At the same time, we will attempt to explain in systems terms what transpired as a result of these interventions, for the overriding concept which has influenced our intervention strategy is that organizations are systems.

We have already dwelt at some length on one implication of this systematic view of organizations—that each organizational improvement effort must be tailored for the requirements of the organization's environment. The second derivation from this view of organizations is that organizational systems are morphogenic and have the capacity to change and develop their structures. We should emphasize again that we are not implying that the organization as an inanimate object accomplishes this. It is, instead, the changing expectations and behavior of individuals which underlies this morphogenic process. Thus, to change the organization, we must change the perceptions and attitudes of organizational members about what is expected of them. This is the primary objective which guides our action planning and implementation in programs such as the one described.

In this particular situation (and in others like it) certain top managers had realized they had a problem. They recognized that there was a significant discrepancy between the desired goals and actual results. To bring about meaningful and lasting organizational changes, we had to accomplish several things, First, it was necessary to help these managers develop a clearer view of their problem and the steps necessary to improve the functioning of the organization. Second, it was necessary to get them committed to taking such action. The diagnostic study and initial feedback sessions provided the vehicle for accomplishing both. As a result of this exposure, the managers later reported that they had obtained a clearer cognitive understanding of their problem and its multiple causes. They had acquired a new set of intellectual tools for thinking about their problem. From their discussions and our interventions they were able to see some action possibilities which could lead to the change goal. The top managers saw data about their own organization which largely matched their intuitive feeling about what was happening; and it was organized conceptually so that they could accept and understand it. As a result, these five top managers became committed to planning and taking action. When they asked for help, they were predisposed to do something, but the diagnostic study and feedback provided a framework and information which they could use to build a shared definition of the problem and the actions required.

Having created a climate for change and at least a broad action plan at the top organizational echelon, we next had to help these top managers transmit to the rest of the organization their expectations that change in certain directions was necessary. This was done through the subsequent feedback session and educational interventions. While the top managers could have stood on a soap box and preached to their subordinates about the need for new behavior patterns, they recognized that the diagnostic study data spoke far more eloquently than they could. This data was a new input of information to the rest of the organizational system that there was a need for changes in certain directions. Like the top managers, other members of the organization later reported that this was precisely what the data feedback accomplished. They said it provided each of them with an understanding of the problems in the organization and their own part in them. The two educational interventions—the simulation of decision-making and the differentiation laboratory—also contributed to creating more understanding of how various individuals were part of the total problem. As they later said, "these sessions provided a mirror to see ourselves." Consequently, there was a general feeling that many individuals had actually altered their behavior. They consciously worked at confronting conflict and at trying to understand the source and meaning of different orientations and outlooks concerning the various functional groups.

Thus, our approach unleashed the potential of the organization to develop new behavior patterns which were consistent with environmental demands, simply by spreading information about the problem behaviors and a more desirable set of behaviors throughout the system. But our approach also encouraged these managers, with this new set of expectations, to make certain formal changes in procedures and task assignments which reinforced the desired behavior pattern. Clear signals were given to members of the integrating group that they should devote more of their time to coordinating long-term research affairs. New decision procedures were developed for handling research projects, which clarified all parties' expectations about how such decisions were to be made. Confrontation was therefore made easier. Action taking of this sort points to another consequence of viewing organizations as systems. This is the fact that expectations and behavior are influenced not only by the predispositions of individuals and the nature of the task but also by formal organizational practices. In this case, only a few of these procedures and assignments were altered. In other situations, more work may be required on these variables. For example, in the Corrugated Container example cited earlier, management became involved in a major redefinition of the role of regional managers and local managers and also changed the formal reward system to emphasize profit performance at the local level.

To summarize, our view of the organizational-development process at this interface is influenced in three ways by the fact that organizations are systems:

1. The objectives of each organizational-development effort, and the action steps, must be tailored to meet the requirements of the organization's environment and the current state of the organization.

2. We view organizational change as the process of changing behavior throughout the system by providing information about the need for change and the required direction of change. This alters the set of expectations held by organization members and motivates them to adopt new behavior patterns.

3. Organizational-development involves operating on all variables influencing behavior—the predispositions of individuals, the nature of the task, and the formal organizational practices. These variables, plus educational intervention, can alter members' expectations and their behavior.

This view contrasts in several ways with that held by others involved in organizational-development work. In concluding this discussion, it is useful to briefly mention some of these contrasts.

## ORGANIZATION DEVELOPMENT
## AT THE GROUP-TO-GROUP INTERFACE:   A CONTRASTING VIEW

In our discussion of organizational development at this interface, we have focused entirely on the relationship between functional groups. However, it is worth noting that this group-to-group interface also can consist of relations between headquarters and field groups, between newly acquired divisions and established divisions, between unions and management, etc. We mention this because, along with other organizational development practitioners, we have also done work on these sorts of relationships. While we do not wish to discuss these here, it should be emphasized that we see the differentiation-and-integration model, and the systematic approach of which it is part, as being fully consistent with efforts to work on these other relationships. Thus, the contrast between our approach and other organizational-development approaches is based not on the settings but rather on differences in emphasis and conceptual tools.

The first of these contrasts in the fact that we have used the systemic differentiation-and-integration model. This approach causes us to develop a particular action-planning and implementation approach for each new setting and to put heavy emphasis on diagnosis. Others who have done organizational-development work at this interface have used more universal approaches and have been less concerned with diagnosis.[4]

In essence, they argue that all organizations need certain characteristics at this interface. Simply stated, these include the development of trust and understanding between groups and the confrontation of conflict. We do not argue that emphasizing these objectives in all cases is wrong. In fact, our model also leads us to see confrontation of conflict as necessary. Where we differ from these other practitioners is in placing emphasis on the requirement for other conflict-management variables which are contingent on environmental demands; on the required state of differentiation; and also on the design of appropriate structural devices for achieving integration. Thus we agree with these other approaches as far as they go, but we feel that a more complete examination of organizations as systems would lead other practitioners to a concern for these other factors in defining the goals of organizational-development efforts.

Since these other organizational development specialists are concerned with this particular set of objectives, it is not surprising that they focus on educational interventions which emphasize face-to-face group process and interpersonal skill. We recognize these as important, but again would go further. From our point of view, such educational approaches are only part of the tools available to bring about organizational development. We have used them in our work such as that described above, but we have also used diagnostic data and have encouraged managers to use other means to alter expectations and behavior (i.e.,

4    See, for example: R. Likert, *The Human Organization*. New York: McGraw-Hill, 1967; R. R. Blake and J. S. Mouton, *The Managerial Grid*. Houston: Gulf Publishing Co., 1964; and C. Argyris, *Interpersonal Competency and Organizational Effectiveness*. Homewood: Richard D. Irwin. 1962.

formal organizational changes, redefinition of tasks, and other educational techniques).

Underlying all of these differences, then, is our view that organizations, as systems carrying out transactions with their environment, are complex and variable. To design organizational-development programs at this or any interface we must first understand both the present state of the organization and the desired goals for improvement. Others doing work in this field seem to recognize intellectually these systemic properties of organization, but, in practice, they put less emphasis on addressing them explicitly.

While these contrasts do exist between our approach and those of others involved in organizational development, it would be misleading to conclude that we are taking completely opposite approaches. For in one important respect there is an important convergence of approach. This is around the basic premise we all hold that an organizational-development program, to be effective at this interface, must gain the commitment and the involvement of the affected managers. They must feel that it is theirs. As outside consultants, we can serve only as catalyst to initiate and keep the effort going. We can suggest action approaches but cannot really take meaningful and lasting action without involving managers within the organization. As we approach an organizational-development project, we view ourselves as experts with certain tools—both diagnostic and action-taking; but our primary objective must be to get organization members involved in this process. Striking the proper balance of being sufficiently involved to get the commitment of organization members but not so involved as to dominate the process is a constant concern which faces all of us involved in developing the complex tools we call organizations. We shall have more to say about these issues in the final chapter, but first we want to turn to the application of our organizational-development approach to the interface between the individual and the organization.

# 5

# THE INDIVIDUAL-AND-ORGANIZATION INTERFACE

Earlier we defined an organization as "the coordination of different activities of individual contributors to carry out planned transactions with the environment." So far, we have dealt with two of the interfaces which this definition suggests—the interface of the organization and its environment, and the interface among groups of individual contributors. The interface between the individual contributor and the organization is the final set of issues upon which we want to focus.

The crucial question at this interface most often raised by managers is how individual contributors can be induced to perform their defined activities. How can we motivate individuals to make the contributions to organization purpose required of them? How can the organization channel and control the behavior of individual contributors in the desired direction? Closely allied is the additional question of how organizational goals can most effectively be communicated to individual contributors so that individuals see the relevance of organization goals to their own personal needs, or stated another way, so that organizational goals and individual needs are complementary, if not congruent, rather than antagonistic. These ways of defining the issue at the individual-organization interface accept the managerial point of view in giving primacy to the achievement of organizational goals. Throughout the bulk of this chapter, we will address the issue in this form, but will later ask where this leaves the individual's needs.

This interface is in a sense the most basic of the three we have considered. For, if an organization is to carry out planned transactions with the several sectors of its environment and is to achieve coordination among its parts, somehow the organization must motivate and control individual contributors so that they effectively perform specialized and coordinated activities. Nevertheless, it is useful to treat this interface separately because, while healthy conditions at this interface are necessary for organizational health at the other interfaces, this alone is not sufficient. Obviously the factors reviewed in the preceding chapters are also necessary for the organization to function at these other interfaces. In this discussion, however, the focus will be on the basic issues of the psychological contract between man and organization and not on how this also relates to the other interface problems already discussed.

Such basic psychological issues do present themselves in all specialized activity groups and at all hierarchical levels. Managers express concern about how to motivate scientists to be more creative, how to induce sales representatives to meet sales quotas, and how to get blue-collar production workers to maintain higher quality standards. They become concerned because employee absenteeism and/or turnover are too high. They wonder which of the multiple packages of monetary and fringe compensations really motivate employees. For example, M. Scott Myers recently has reported on the efforts of the Texas Instrument Co. to understand and develop this interface for a wide variety of employees—from scientists, engineering and manufacturing supervisors, to technicians and workers on the assembly line.[1]

These issues are not limited to the lower and middle levels of the organization but are equally pertinent for top management. In our own experience, one of the authors has been involved in helping the proprietors of a family-owned business consider ways of working out a psychological transaction with the professional managers in the firm so they would be more motivated to contribute to the long-term growth of the organization even though they were barred from ownership equity. These same issues are at the heart of one of the thorniest problems faced by the top corporate management of the so-called "conglomerate" companies. These corporate managers are plagued by the issue of how to motivate the chief

---

[1]    M. S. Myers, "Who Are Your Motivated Workers?," Harv. Bus. Rev., January and February, 1964.

executives of newly acquired divisions. The division managers frequently were the former owners and have been made independently wealthy by the acquisition transaction. These corporate managers are asking, in effect, how we can continue to keep the division executives motivated toward divisional growth and profits when the value they personally place on economic incentive may have been substantially reduced.

In all of these instances, managers are usually very much aware of the symptoms of the problem. They can point to the lack of effort or results or to absenteeism or turnover. However, quite often their explanation is that the individual contributors involved have a character weakness: they lack motivation. But managers who offer this explanation fail to see its basic fallacy. The fact that individuals are not motivated to accomplish organizational goals does not mean they lack motivation. It simply means that they are motivated to do something other than work toward organizational ends. For example, the fact that the workers in Roethlisberger's and Dickson's study of the bank wiring room restricted output could not be cited as proof that they lacked motivation.[2] On the contrary, they were highly motivated to develop elaborate mechanisms to restrict production output. Similarly, the former owner of a newly acquired division of a diversified firm does not suddenly lose his motivation. He is still motivated, but he directs his effort toward his golf score or investing in the stock market.

Thus, one of the difficulties facing managers who are concerned with problems at this interface is that they lack the tools to obtain even a rudimentary understanding of the issues of individual motivation. They can identify symptoms but not causes, and thus are at a loss to develop a meaningful diagnosis and action plan which would allow them to rearrange the organization-individual transaction so that individual and organizational goals are at least complementary. The first step, therefore, for persons doing organizational development work at this interface is to provide a set of conceptual tools which can be applied to the kinds of problems we have mentioned.

## Relevant Motivational Concepts

Of the three interface issues that we are considering, there is little doubt that we have available more concepts, tools and theories for dealing with the individual-organization interface. But the availability of these concepts

2    F. J. Roethlisberger and W. J. Dickson, *Management and the Worker.* Cambridge: Harvard University Press, 1939.

is not an unmixed blessing. The difficulty is that the wide body of literature on individual motivation in organizational settings offers a variety of explanations, often contradictory, of what motivates individuals to make contributions to organizational goals. While space precludes a comprehensive review of even the major conceptual positions, Schein has provided an interesting and concise summary, which provides the flavor of several major approaches.[3]

The first assumption about individual motivation which Schein discusses is the idea that man is basically rational-economic. According to this view, man is primarily motivated by economic rewards. Such economic rewards are controlled by the organization. Consequently, the psychological contract between individual and organization is very simple—effort in exchange for money. Man's feelings about work, other individuals in the organization, or the organization itself are essentially irrational. Through management action and the design of the organization, these feelings must be prevented from interfering with the rational-economic contract between individual and organization. As Schein also points out, these ideas have been put to work historically in a large number of industrial settings and even today are widely accepted. To a certain extent, they are successful in that they induce individual contributors to work toward organizational goals. But their essential shortcoming is that they fail to recognize a number of other human needs.

As Schein points out, the observation of this shortcoming by Elton Mayo and his colleagues led to the development of another approach to individual motivation in organizations. This approach placed emphasis on man's social needs. The need for belonging was seen as providing the basic motivation for individuals to work. An exaggerated and idealized statement of this view of the psychological contract individuals would prefer with the organization would be satisfaction of social needs in exchange for individual effort. According to this view, man's emphasis on social needs is a result of the rationalization of work, which has reduced the intrinsic meaning of work for the individual. Under these conditions, management needs to recognize the existence of peer groups as a source of powerful satisfaction for individuals. If the shared expectations of members of a work group do not support organizational goals, the social controls of the work group can be a powerful countervailing force to management's efforts to use financial rewards and organizational controls

3    E. H. Schein, *Organizational Psychology*. Englewood Cliffs, N.J.: Prentice-Hall, 1965, pp. 47-63.

to achieve organizational goals. This view of individual motivation stimulated a large number of research studies into the topic. While, according to Schein, these studies lent general support to the assumption "that man is socially motivated in his organizational life," they also. . . . "caution us not to overgeneralize. Though the rational economic model of man is clearly not very general, we cannot claim clear evidence for the universality of social man, either."[4]

Other behavioral scientists shared Mayo's conclusion that work in organizations, particularly industrial organizations, had lost much of its intrinsic value. Schein indicates that these researchers found that "this loss of meaning is not related so much to man's social needs, however, as to man's inherent need to use his capacities and skills in a mature and productive way."[5] Psychologists like Argyris, Maslow, and McGregor, therefore, developed a third set of motivational assumptions which Schein has labeled "self-actualizing man." The assumptions underlying this approach, according to Maslow, are that man's needs are arranged in a hierarchy—needs for safety or survival, social needs, needs for self esteem, needs for autonomy, and needs for self-actualization, that is, the opportunity for man to use all his resources. As the lower-level needs (safety and social, etc.) are satisfied, man becomes interested in satisfying the higher-order needs (autonomy and self-actualization). According to this view, the ultimate psychological contract between man and organization could be written as safety, social contact, self-esteem, autonomy, and self-actualization in exchange for individual effort. The problem, according to this view, however, is that while man ultimately seeks independence and self-actualization, the organizational context places him in a position of dependency and constraint which prevents him from satisfying these higher-order needs.

Schein concludes his discussion of self-actualizing man by pointing to the limits of this view. "There is clear evidence that such needs [higher-order needs] are important in the higher levels of organizational members like managers and professionals on the staff. It is not clear how characteristic these needs are of the lower-level employee, although many of the problems which were interpreted to be examples of thwarted social needs could as easily be reinterpreted to be instances of thwarted needs for challenge and meaning."[6]

4    *Ibid.*, pg. 56
5    *Ibid.*, pg. 56.
6    *Ibid.*, pg. 59.

At this point, we have reviewed a sufficient number of approaches to understanding the individual-organization interface so that the reader can sense the dilemma these approaches pose for organizational-development activity. Accepting any one of them at the expense of the others could have a profound effect on one's diagnosis of the situation and on subsequent action plans and implementation steps. Not only do they provide conflicting views in what they consider, but they also leave untouched major areas and issues which our systemic approach indicates would be relevant to consider. None of these approaches takes into account the variable nature of individual tasks or the multitude of possible variations in formal organizational factors. They fail to recognize that the predispositions of different individuals may vary. In essence, as Schein has pointed out, "organization and management theory has tended toward simplified and generalized conceptions of man."[7]

Schein's answer to this dilemma is to take a fourth approach which he has labeled as "complex man." This is basically the same direction which we have followed in our own work. It builds upon the historical contributions of the earlier approaches discussed above, but it also takes account of the fact that each of these approaches tells only part of the story, and it utilizes more recent empirical research findings.

The conceptual framework which we utilize at this interface recognizes the complexity of man and the factors that influence his motivation to contribute to organizational goals. But it also provides a framework for bringing some order out of the theoretical confusions which we have reviewed and out of the basic complexity of the problem which organizational development at this interface poses. This conceptual scheme is built upon a number of recent research findings which indicate that an individual can usefully be conceived of as a system of biological needs, psychological motives, values, and perceptions.[8]

The individual's system operates so as to maintain its internal balance in the face of the demands placed upon it by external forces. In essence, this internal system develops in response to the individual's basic need to solve the problems presented by his external environment. For the infant, the problems which must be solved are the essential ones of securing food,

7  *Ibid.*, pg. 60.

8  See, for example, Schein, *Ibid.*, pp. 60-65; J. A. Seiler, *A Systems Approach to Organizational Behavior* (Homewood, Ill: Richard D. Irwin, 1967), pp. 51-81; K. Meninger *et al.*, *The Vital Balance* (New York: The Viking Press, 1963), especially pp. 76-124.

warmth, etc., and relating to parents and siblings. For the older child the problems become more complex, dealing with a wider array of others—teachers, playmates, peers in school, etc., and more complex objects, intellectual knowledge, more complicated toys, etc. This same problem-solving need is evident in adults in organizational life. In this setting the problems posed may consist of dealing with superiors, subordinates, or peers, and of performing specific tasks. But this basic problem-solving need, or what White has termed a need for a sense of competence or mastery, is the same.[9]

The relevance of this problem-solving view of the individual system to the individual-organization interface is suggested by the work of Herzberg and of Myers.[10] For example, in their work at Texas Instruments, Myers and his colleagues found that organization members in many jobs at several levels were motivated by the challenge of and opportunity for accomplishment on their jobs. The intrinsic involvement in the work and the sense of accomplishment derived were more important motivators than such other factors as social rewards, status, physical conditions, and even economic rewards. Herzberg earlier had made a similar point by drawing the distinction between hygienic factors (physical conditions, supervisory policies, wages and fringe benefits, etc.) and motivating factors (the nature of the work itself.) Herzberg's basic point, upon which Myers and his colleagues have built, is that an individual's real motivation comes from a sense of task accomplishment. These hygienic factors are so labeled because they do not motivate but only represent actions taken to prevent dissatisfaction. Basically, the work of Herzberg and Myers suggests that individuals, in their transactions with the organizational setting, are motivated by a desire to use their problem-solving abilities.

But to apply this problem-solving view of man to organizational-development activities, we need a more comprehensive view of the characteristics of the individual system. The statement that man is motivated by a need to master the problems he confronts is too broad and general. It is subject to the same criticism that Schein leveled at other motivational and management theories. To make this view of man operational in the context of specific organizational situations, we need to elaborate on how the individual system develops. As we suggested above, this transpires as the individual strives to master the external world. The

9    R. White, "Ego and Reality in Psychoanalytic Theory," Psych. Iss., Vol. III, No. 3, Monograph No. 11, 1963, pp. 24-43.

10    See, for example, F. J. Herzberg et al., The Motivation to Work. New York: Wiley, 1959; and Myers, Op. cit.

pattern of motives, values, and perceptions which develops in a particular individual personality system is the product of the interaction of the biological characteristics of the individual and the development experience the individual encounters from infancy through adult life. This means that, while all individuals strive to solve the problems confronting them, the variety of different experiences leads each individual system to develop differently. This process continues even in adult years, although, because of the need to maintain an internal balance, the growth and development is always in an internally consistent direction. In spite of the interesting work being done in the area of personality development,[11] it is too complex a topic to pursue in depth here. For our purposes, the essential points are two:

1. Different individual systems develop with different patterns of needs, values and perceptions.

2. Individual systems are not static, but continue to develop as they encounter new problem experiences.

The fact that each individual system will have unique characteristics is one of the reasons this interface is so complex. Yet this complexity can be handled, if we recognize that our primary interest is in the development of organizational systems, not in understanding each individual system. This does not mean that we should totally ignore individual differences, but rather that we should focus on differences among individual systems, which are meaningful in understanding the relationships between individual contributors and the organization.

While psychologists have provided a great many concepts and constructs for categorizing the variables in individual systems, we have found it useful to employ three major constructs to describe these systems:

*Perceptions:* the information the system takes in about its environment.

*Values:* the set of beliefs about what is right and wrong, important and unimportant, which are consciously held.

*Motives:* the underlying drives or needs which develop unconsciously as the individual experiences success and failure in mastering his environment.

11   See, for example, R. White, *Lives in Progress* (New York: Holt, Rinehart and Winston, 1966); and E. H. Eriksen, *Childhood and Society* (New York: W. W. Newton, 1950).

As has been suggested, these three variables are highly interrelated. For example, what an individual perceives in a particular situation is influenced by his values and his motives. The development of motives and values in turn is influenced by the process of perception which determines what information the system takes in. These perceptual mechanisms which filter information in and out are crucial in enabling the healthy individual system to maintain its balance, while still learning from new experiences.

In accomplishing organizational-development work, one must rely heavily on all three of these constructs. But since we are chiefly concerned with issues of motivation at this interface, the most important variables to understand are often the motives themselves. Again, psychologists have provided an abundance of categories to delineate differences in motive patterns within the personality system. In fact, the list seems endless. However, one way of categorizing motives which seems particularly useful for our purposes is provided by McClelland when he identifies three important motives: need for achievement, need for affiliation, and need for power.[12]

Need for achievement is defined as the need for competitive success measured against a personal standard of excellence. Need for affiliation is defined as the need for warm, friendly, compassionate relationships with others. Need for power is defined as the need to control or influence others. As we would expect, McClelland and his colleagues have found that different individuals have different levels of these motives. Some individuals have a greater need for achievement, others a stronger need for affiliation, and still others a stronger need for power. While one motive may be dominant for particular individuals, it does not mean that the others are nonexistent. The other motives, however, are somewhat less important.

The relationship between these three motives and the need for problem-solving is not difficult to comprehend. In fact, it seems that the problem-solving need basically underlies these three motives and others which have not yet been so precisely identified and measured. As the individual system strives to master problems, certain behaviors turn out to be consistently rewarding; that is, they provide solutions to the problems the individual faces. Consequently, the next time the individual needs to solve a problem he tries the same pattern of behavior again. Over time, as some of these patterns are consistently rewarding, the individual learns to rely on them. Thus, we say that a person is highly motivated to compete

12   D. McClelland, *The Achieving Society*. New York: D. Van Nostrand, 1961.

against a standard of excellence (need for achievement), or has a higher need for warm friendly relations (need for affiliation), etc. As a result of this learning process, different individuals develop the different patterns of these motives already described.

The discussion so far has focused on a crude description of how these motives develop over time and how the person's behavior in a particular organizational situation is not only a function of the characteristics of his individual system but also is a result of the problems and challenges he perceives in the organizational setting. The nature of these challenges is affected not only by what the individual system perceives but also by the reality of the problems the organization provides. The reality of the problems, as we suggested in Chapters 1 and 2, is shaped by the expectations of others, by the nature of the task which the individual is required to perform, and by the formal organizational variables, such as supervisory style, rewards and punishments, rules, control procedures, etc., with which he is confronted. The individual system, others' expectations, the task and formal organizational variables interact to form the individual's view of what is expected of him by the organization. The interaction of these variables defines the kind of bargain the individual and the organization have made.

To state it differently, how an individual is motivated to behave in a specific organizational position is a function of both the developmental history of his individual system and the nature of the current organizational context. Each individual is motivated to behave in the current situation in accordance with the past behavior patterns which have helped him master his environment. When he meets a given organizational or job situation, his personal history causes him to perceive certain aspects of the current situation as potentially satisfying and others as less so. Thus, whether a person behaves as a high achiever, an affiliator, or as one who is more power-motivated depends not only on the strength of these inherent motives, but also upon the extent to which he perceives that these or any other underlying motives will be satisfied in the particular setting.

This view of the relationship at the organization-individual interface can be diagrammed as in Fig. 5.[13]

This conceptual scheme helps us to see two opportunities for developing this interface. One lies in developing individual systems to

13   This conception is consistent with Atkinson's view. See J. W. Atkinson (ed.), *Motives in Fantasy, Action, and Society.* Princeton, N.J.: D. Van Nostrand, Inc., 1958; especially pp. 228–305.

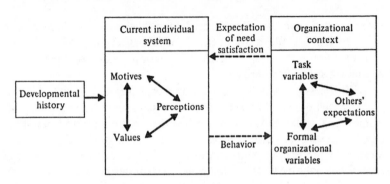

**Figure 5**

make them more consistent with the rewards available from task and organizational factors. This can be accomplished through influencing perceptions and values and through motivation training,[14] or through the criteria used to select and promote individuals. The other opportunity is to alter the task or organizational variables so that they will afford a higher expectation of need satisfaction. But the essential fact which needs emphasis is that an individual's motivation to make a contribution to organizational goals requires that such behavior fulfill his important needs, whether these be achievement, power, affiliation, or some other. In essence, organizational development at this interface must work toward the objective of obtaining a fit between individual needs and the behavior required of the individual to accomplish organizational goals.

As we have already indicated, in seeking this objective we do not become overly concerned with differences among the needs of individual organization members. Instead, we have found it useful to identify the behaviors which are required to perform a particular set of tasks effectively and then to determine what individual characteristics are most often associated with this behavior. For example, in attempting to achieve more effective performance on the part of "integrators" in an organization, it was learned, from an analysis of the task and an examination of the personality characteristics of more and less effective performers in this job, that a relatively high need for affiliation, along with moderately high achievement, was associated with effectiveness. These jobs provided a high

14    For a detailed statement on motivation training, see D. C. McClelland, "Toward a Theory of Motive Acquisition," *Amer. Psych.*, Vol. 20. No. 5, May, 1965.

expectation of meeting these needs, and people with this need pattern found these jobs interesting and performed more effectively.[15]

Taking such an approach to developing this interface means placing heavy emphasis on diagnosis. We need to identify in what activity groups problems exist at this interface. What are the attributes of these jobs and what behavior leads to effective performance? What individual system characteristics are most likely to motivate individuals to perform this sort of task effectively? Are the expectations of others, the organizational relationships, rewards, and controls likely to work toward increasing the expectation of need attainment, or will they operate in the opposite direction? Such a diagnosis provides a picture of the problem issues at this interface and the direction in which change is required. From it the organizational-development consultant and/or the managers concerned can develop an action plan.

## ORGANIZATION DEVELOPMENT AT THIS INTERFACE

To understand more fully how this scheme can be used to develop this organizational interface, it is helpful to provide a few examples. The three examples we have chosen all involve sales organizations. While we might have selected examples concerned with research scientists, production managers, or top corporate executives, we have decided to use these examples for three reasons. First, they occurred quite recently, and we, or our colleagues, have fairly complete data about what transpired. Second, by focusing on two of these sales situations, we can emphasize how critical it is that a careful analysis be made of the behavior required to perform the task. It is not enough to say "the task is selling, therefore. . . ." Third, two of the examples we will discuss provide an important contrast in intervention strategy. We will come back to this contrast shortly, but let us start by focusing on two examples where the intervention approach was almost classically diagnostic. That is, the consultant made a study of problems at this interface and provided his analysis and recommendations to the top managers involved.

The first of these efforts was conducted in the medical division of a major diversified company. This division engaged in the manufacture,

15  P. R. Lawrence and J. W. Lorsch, "New Management Job: The Integrator," Harv. Bus. Rev., November-December, 1967.

sales, distribution, and service of highly technical (mechanical, electrical, and electronic) equipment used in hospital operating rooms. Although some smaller items of equipment in the division's product line sold for only $5,000 to $20,000, very large complete systems might cost from $150,000 to $200,000.

This project, which was undertaken by the Behavioral Science Center of Cambridge, Mass., under the direction of our colleague Dr. George Litwin, was initiated by the company's personnel staff. Their interest was to help this division's management understand the more effective sales performance by a certain district sales office. (The division's sales organization was divided into three regions, each with approximately ten district offices. A typical district had six to eight salesmen and sixteen to twenty servicemen who installed and serviced the equipment.) This study, it was hoped, would lead to the development of other sales offices into more effective units.

In initial contacts with the top managers in the division, the consultant learned that these managers had only vague ideas of the factors which led to effective sales performance. They associated top sales performance with hard work and effort. As the consultants carried out their initial conversations, they also became aware that neither they nor these managers had a clear understanding of what the selling task really involved or what the personality characteristics of effective salesmen were likely to be. Additionally, the consultants learned that there was a great deal of variation in the management styles and organizational practices among the various district offices.

Consequently, they and the division managers worked out arrangements to conduct a comparative study of four highly effective district offices and four average offices, judged by the company's usual measures of sales performance. Through interviews with salesmen and managers, the consultants intended to obtain a clearer view of the nature of the selling task and to learn about the management style of district managers. To measure the characteristics of individuals, two instruments were used. Thematic Apperception Tests (TAT) were used to measure basic motives (need for achievement, affiliation and power). The California Psychological Inventory (CPI) was utilized to measure several other behavioral characteristics (leadership, maturity, drive, and flexibility). Finally, the consultants administered a questionnaire developed by Litwin to measure the "organization climate."[16] This instrument is designed to elicit

16   G. H. Litwin and R. A. Stringer, Jr., *Motivation and Organizational Climate.* Boston: Division of Research, Harvard Business School, 1968.

individuals' perceptions of the structure in which they work, along these dimensions: structure, responsibility, risk, standards, rewards and support, and friendly team spirit. Thus, the consultants had designed a study which provided data about three system variables (task, individual systems, and organizational variables) in each of the eight district offices studied.

From their interviews with salesmen and managers, the consultants developed a very clear understanding of the task of selling this complex equipment and what it involved. They learned that the selling task with a particular customer could involve many years of effort. In the first phase of the selling task, which might last from one to fifteen years, the salesman had to meet the influential doctors and administrators of the hospital(s). He had to learn about their requirements and, most important, had to develop their trust and confidence in him. This first phase was followed by a relatively short entrepreneurial selling phase (six months to three years) in which the salesman made a detailed study of the specific needs, planned and made a sales presentation and, hopefully, closed the sale. Even though the sale was closed, the salesman still had to continue working with the customer through what the consultants termed the Service/Recall phase. This phase, which might last fifteen to twenty-five years, involved overseeing the delivery and installation of equipment and also subsequent servicing of equipment. During this phase, the salesman was required to make periodic "recalls" to the customer to make certain that he was satisfied with the equipment and service and also to maintain the relationship for future orders.

Two aspects of this description of the selling task are worthy of emphasis. First, the last phase required that the salesman be able to collaborate effectively with the service personnel in his district. Second, the long-term relationships involved between salesman and customer and the long period typically required before a sale could be consummated meant that the salesman had to be satisfied with working without immediate indication of results. The real source of satisfaction during these periods had to be derived from the experience of building and maintaining relationships with customers. The significance of these two facts will become apparent as we look at the data which the consultants gathered on the organization and the individuals.

With regard to individual system characteristics, the consultants obtained results which at first seemed surprising. Studies by McClelland and others had found that successful salesmen tended to be very high on need for achievement. Consequently, this was what the consultants thought they would find in this setting. While need for achievement was the dominant motive for salesmen in both average and outstanding districts, the salesmen in the average offices scored higher on need for achievement than did those in outstanding offices. This surprised the consultants initially. Even more surprising initially was the fact that in need for affiliation the salesmen in the outstanding districts scored higher than those in the average districts. (There was no meaningful difference between the two groups in need for power). On the CPI measures the salesmen in the outstanding districts scored higher on capacity for leadership drive through independence and flexibility.

While we indicated these data were initially unexpected, the consultants quickly began to see the pattern which was emerging. Using roughly the set of concepts we described above, they recognized that the task provided a high expectation of need satisfaction for a person with a stronger need for affiliation. As suggested above, this was the only need which would be satisfied during the long periods of relation-building. While the need for achievement was satisfied as sales were eventually closed, the opportunity to satisfy their need for affiliation motivated the salesmen in outstanding offices to work at building long-term relationships. The fact that they sought achievement through independence was obviously also important, since much of this effort had to be conducted autonomously, with minimum supervision.

There was also another reason that a higher need for affiliation was suited to this particular task. Since the salesmen had to collaborate with service personnel during the final phases of the selling task, it was important for them to gain intrinsic satisfaction from the opportunity to work closely with others. Related to this was their capacity to take a leadership role in their relations with servicemen. The importance of this factor can better be understood after we have reviewed the data collected about organizational variables.

Along all six dimensions of organization climate measured (structure, responsibility, risk, standards, rewards and support, and friendly team spirit), the members of the outstanding districts perceived that their organizations were more favorable than did members of the average districts. The largest differences in perception were in friendly team spirit, which would be conducive to creating expectations of satisfying a need for affiliation among sales personnel and between sales and service personnel, as well as with customers. Other major differences were in structure, risk, standards, and rewards and support. All of these, according to Litwin's research, are important in creating expectations of satisfaction of the need for achievement.[17]

17.  *Ibid.*

As we might expect from these data, the interview data about management style indicated that managers in outstanding offices set higher standards, provided more coaching, and were more participative and consultative. In sum, the data about these organizational variables indicated that the outstanding offices provided a setting in which sales personnel would find a greater expectation of satisfying both their need for achievement and, most importantly, their need for affiliation.

From all of these data, we can understand the sorts of conclusions the consultants reached. Namely, that for a district to be outstanding it had to have organizational practices and management styles which created an expectation of satisfying both a need for achievement, which is associated with most sales tasks, and, especially critical in this situation, a need for affiliation. Having such organization variables was consistent with the task requirements outlined above. As the salesmen in the outstanding districts went about mastering the problems of their environment, they saw high expectations of need satisfaction along these two dimensions. Apparently, these needs were important to them and the possibility for satisfying them motivated these salesmen to work toward organizational goals.

Having collected this data and organized it within this conceptual framework, the consultants reported their findings to division management. Their action recommendations focused heavily on developing and training district managers, for if the management style of the district managers in the average offices could be altered toward setting higher standards, acting as coaches and being more participative, their salesmen would have increased expectations that their needs for achievement and affiliation would be satisfied. They might therefore be more highly motivated to behave in ways which would lead to accomplishing organizational goals. In this regard, it is important to emphasize that the data about the motive patterns of salesmen in outstanding offices was not taken as an indication that they necessarily had higher need for affiliation—only that the interaction between their needs and the organizational variables activated this need more strongly.

As a result of this diagnostic study, the division management is developing a management-training program which it is hoped will affect the styles of district managers in the desired direction. Obviously, however, there are other system variables which the consultants could have focused on (e.g., eliminating the commission-compensation scheme for salesmen, de-emphasizing short-term sales targets in management information reports, etc.). The consultants, however, chose to focus on management training, because many of these other variables were more difficult to change. We mention them here because they are available variables which must be considered in taking action at this interface of the organization.

The second example with which we want to deal affords us an opportunity to see how some of these other organizational variables can be altered to improve the relationship between individual and organization. The problem in this instance was one in which one of the authors was directly involved. The management of this firm, a medium-sized manufacturer of women's sportswear with about thirty salesmen, felt that a number of these representatives were not performing up to par.[18] After some discussion, it was agreed that a study should be undertaken to learn more about the individual task and organizational variables involved. Rather than utilize more sophisticated data-gathering techniques such as those described above, it was decided to rely completely on interviews with salesmen and management personnel. The reason for this was that the level of sophistication about behavioral-science techniques in the organization was extremely low. We were concerned that the use of psychological tests and questionnaires would alienate members of the organization and unnecessarily complicate the action-planning and implementation stages. Obviously, decisions such as this are highly subjective, but it does indicate the sort of trade-offs between diagnostic precision and complications in action phases which persons involved in organizational development must make. We will have more to say about this later.

Without dwelling on the diagnostic phase at length, let us briefly summarize the conclusions we drew from interviews with both outstanding salesmen and those performing below par (as identified by top management). First, the task of a salesman in this organization was defined as follows: to work with the retail store, to not only get the merchandise into the store but also to move it out of the store. The salesman had to work with store merchandising personnel to get an appropriate selection of merchandise into the store, to have the merchandise properly displayed, and to motivate store personnel to give his merchandise as much or more attention than competing lines. This meant that the salesman was required to work with store personnel to determine appropriate orders, arrange sales training, check inventory, etc. We might add that this view of the selling task was at odds with the traditional view in the organization that the salesman was to concentrate simply on writing orders.

18    Samantha Sportswear Case. Copyright by the President and Fellows of Harvard College, 1968.

Second, with regard to the individual characteristics of outstanding salesmen, we found that they did conceive of the task as described above. Further, they indicated that they got satisfaction from building business in the stores. They enjoyed watching the volume grow, and seeing the merchandise move out of the store. These salesmen indicated that they were willing to take certain risks in guiding the store personnel in the selection of merchandise. They did these things because they seemed to realize that they were essential to get the feedback of growing sales volume which they found rewarding. In the terms we have been using, these outstanding salesmen demonstrated a higher need for achievement than their less effective colleagues. For the less effective salesmen, the main satisfaction was in the commission check. Money for them was an end in itself. For the outstanding salesmen, however, the motivating factor was clearly a drive to accomplish and achieve a growing business in their territory.

The organizational variables to control and motivate salesmen in this situation were few. Commission accounts were settled on a periodic basis. Salesmen were called to meetings to familiarize them with the product line at the beginning of each of the four selling seasons. Beyond this, contact with management was sporadic and occurred largely when special problems arose or when a new man was started in the territory.

This diagnosis led us to the conclusion that the key to obtaining higher motivation for the salesmen was to provide a higher expectation of satisfying his need for achievement. While the outstanding salesmen seemed to have sufficiently strong need for achievement, so that they found this expectation in the intrinsic nature of the task, most of the salesmen did not. Therefore, we recommended certain modifications in the organizational practices connected with the sales force. While we advised a continuation of the exclusively commission compensation scheme, we urged management to begin formalized procedure for setting goals jointly with salesmen, for measuring performance against goals, and for evaluating such performance. This recommendation is consistent with McClelland's conclusion that need for achievement is stimulated by feedback about performance against established standards.

We also recommended that in selecting new salesmen, attention be paid to the achievement drive of the applicant as one important selection criteria. Finally, we urged the initiation of systematic coaching by sales management and formalized training to help the salesmen develop an understanding of how and why the retail store bought. This, we felt, was crucial, because while the outstanding salesmen had this understanding and used it to accomplish their self-established goals, the less effective salesmen did not. Setting goals to motivate them would simply be frustrating unless the means to achieve the goals were also provided.

In this situation, then, we recommended changing formal organizational variables in order to create for the individual a higher expectation of need satisfaction. By doing this, and by influencing his behavior through more frequent coaching and training, we hoped to influence him to become more active in pursuing organizational goals. In essence, the psychological contract would become need satisfaction through individual effort.

These two examples present an interesting contrast, which gets to the heart of our approach to organizational development at this interface. On the surface, both situations presented similar problems: how to motivate sales representatives. Too many managers and organization-development specialists would recommend the same treatments for both: salesman training, a new incentive scheme, a better psychological test for selecting salesmen, etc. However, the diagnostic studies conducted in each of these situations clearly suggest that while the same variables might be manipulated in the two cases, the directions and objectives of altering these organizational variables would be quite different. In the medical-equipment organization, the objective would be to provide a setting which tended to arouse both affiliative and achievement motives. In the sportswear case, the goal would be to stimulate need for achievement.

Again, at this interface, then, we see clearly the reason for our emphasis on careful diagnosis as an intrinsic part of any organizational-development effort. What happens at this interface, like the others discussed in previous chapters, is a result of an interdependent system of task, individual, and organizational factors. To understand the goals of organizational development and how to achieve them, it is first mandatory to understand this system. Then the practitioner, whether he be a member of the organization or an outsider, is in a position to more clearly delineate an action plan and to implement it.

However, it would be misleading to leave the impression that once the diagnosis is made the action and implementation steps will follow easily. This is no more the case at this interface than it was at the others described above. In fact, our experience at this interface indicates that the problems of gaining acceptance of diagnostic conclusions and converting them to action may be even more difficult than at the other interfaces. For example, in the sportswear firm, a great deal of resistance to the conclusion of our diagnosis was encountered initially. The top managers had strongly held beliefs about the power of financial incentives as motivators. Any suggestion that less concrete factors, such as goal-setting, training, etc., might improve motivation ran contrary to their own assumptions about human motivation. (To a lesser extent, the consultants in the medical equipment firm encountered similar difficulties.) After a series of meetings with these top managers, we were able to work through the meaning of the data and to obtain their involvement in most of the action steps suggested above. Nevertheless, their doubts about the validity of the data linger, and their involvement in action-planning has certainly been less enthusiastic than that we encountered in working at the group-to-group interface.

Differences in the nature of problems and data at these two interfaces seems to account for this difficulty. At the group-to-group interface, the problems are more visible. The behavior associated with unresolved intergroup disputes is observable. Top managers often can actually see it. As a result, diagnostic data at that interface has more face validity. It can be related to the experience of the managers involved. At the individual-organization interface, managers sense that people are not motivated, but they cannot see or understand the factors leading to this lack of motivation. In addition, as we suggested earlier, they often have strongly held assumptions about motivation. For these reasons, the data reported in diagnostic studies at this interface are not so quickly accepted. Yet, with patience and ingenuity, a working through of these doubts can be achieved so that managers will begin to act on the data.

## EMPHASIS ON IMPLEMENTATION

There is also, however, another approach to developing this interface which we and others have used and which makes the problems of initiating action somewhat less acute. In this approach, less emphasis is placed on diagnosis and more on implementation. For example, in recent work with a marketing firm involved in selling a wide variety of consumer products to variety and chain stores, we and our colleagues used such an approach.

The management of this firm approached us with the vague feeling that they needed "human-relations" training for their sales management personnel. They proposed a one-week seminar. In our preliminary discussions, we emphasized that we would be interested in such a program only if it could be tailored to their problems. The top managers agreed, and we spent only two days interviewing them about current organizational problems. From these interviews, we ascertained that while there were several sets of problems, the major ones occurred at the individual-organization interface. How to motivate district managers and salesmen; how to communicate company goals to them; how to evaluate their performance and coach them in improving their performance, etc. While these problems varied in intensity and in kind, they were present in all four of the company's product divisions.

With this background, we planned a week-long session intended to initiate an organizational-improvement effort at this interface. More specifically, our objectives were three:

1. To get the managers (approximately fifty from the president down to and including district sales managers) to specifically identify the organizational problems with which they were concerned.

2. To provide some simple concepts and our own expertise to develop their understanding of these problems.

3. To get them to develop and begin to implement action plans.

While we intentionally did not make a systematic diagnosis of task, individual, and organizational factors, we did work on the educated guess that effective performance of their sales task would be obtained by providing an expectation of satisfaction of need for achievement. We also were prepared to alter this assumption if the managers' own diagnosis indicated that this was necessary.

Working with this assumption, the one-week program was designed to first give the managers a chance, through self-scored questionnaires and discussions, to evaluate their own organization.

The initial day of the program was spent arriving at a diagnosis of the organization. Specifically, the managers were asked to determine how the organization's culture and their own management style moved them to deal with problems at the various interfaces we have discussed. Were they seeking integrative or confronting types of solutions which worked problems until a solution was found? Were they using force and power to solve problems? Or were they smoothing and avoiding problems? Although this was admittedly a crude set of categories, it did serve as a catalyst to get the managers to examine the problems in their organization. While problems were identified at the organization-and-environment and group-to-group interfaces, the major problems, as our preliminary reading had indicated, were identified as being at the individual-organization interface. The managers realized they were not being effective in motivating subordinate managers and salesmen and in communicating organizational goals to them.

After this problem-identification phase, two days were devoted to introducing conceptual material and to discussing cases related to issues of leadership style and the design of goal-setting and communication procedures. All of this was done in a manner consistent with our assumption that the tasks to be performed required an achievement-oriented system, for the managers' own diagnosis supported this set of assumptions.

With this brief conceptual background, we asked the management groups from each division to develop a proposal to deal with one of the problems identified. All chose to work on the organization-individual interface. For example, one division's management described a preliminary procedure for goal-setting and evaluation of performance against goals. Another division devoted attention to revising its measurement system to provide feedback to district managers and salesmen.

While all of these proposals were preliminary and very crude, they all were enthusiastically endorsed by most of the managers. They were their own creation. They had recognized the need for them and had used their limited behavioral-science tools to design them. This commitment of the managers concerned is the chief benefit from this approach. In our experience, this implementation approach does obtain commitment more quickly than the diagnostic approaches mentioned earlier. Its drawback is that it uses only crude behavioral-science tools and thus may miss some opportunities that a more sophisticated diagnosis and action plan would uncover. This sort of trade-off between the sophisticated use of behavioral-science tools and management commitment is a dilemma with which organization-development specialists are constantly faced, and we see no easy solutions to it.


## SUMMARY

We can draw certain conclusions about organizational development at this interface. Our basic objective at this interface, like the others discussed in prior chapters, is to make managers aware of the nature of the system of variables influencing the relationship between individual and organization. To what extent do the individual's system, task characteristics, and organizational variables interact to produce behavior which rewards the individual and accomplishes organizational goals? How can any or *all* of these variables be altered to motivate the individual to engage more fully in accomplishing organizational goals because he finds this behavior rewarding?

While we have pursued these questions in terms of sales organizations, the same issues present themselves for other groups of individual contributors and the same concepts are relevant. For example, if one is concerned about motivating scientists, he must understand the nature of the creative task he wants them to perform, the values and motives central to the scientists' individual systems, and the organizational variables which are intended to control and motivate the scientists. Do these organizational variables offer an expectation of reward for a person who has scientific values and who seeks to express these values through achievement in an industrial setting?

If one is concerned about the motivation of production employees, the same factors are relevant even though the specific situation is considerably different. In production assignments, a diagnosis may reveal that the task requirements are too restricted and too simple to engage any of the problem-solving motives of the individuals employed. In such an instance, serious consideration of job enlargement is indicated. Can the task be technically redesigned so that its intrinsic features engage more of the motives of the individuals involved? Questions such as these are the ones which this approach to developing this interface seeks to answer. Beyond this it enables the managers to develop action steps which create a higher expectation of reward for the individual if he performs the organizationally required behavior.

But, as the final portion of our discussion has suggested, putting so much emphasis on diagnosis at this interface does have its drawbacks. Managers often find it difficult to accept these diagnoses and to act on them. The answer may rest partially in the interpersonal skill of the organization-development specialist as he works to help managers to understand and accept the diagnosis. Alternatively, it may rest in placing more emphasis on obtaining management commitment and less on elegant diagnoses. We will explore this issue in our final chapter, but for now we can again emphasize that the complexity at this interface can be understood only by some sort of prior diagnosis and by using this as the basis for action steps. Otherwise, the organizational-development effort is very likely to flounder in a morass of generalizations and panaceas which are irrelevant in the particular setting. Furthermore, if action is taken on the basis of a careful diagnosis, it can increase the degree of fit between the goals of the organization and the needs and aspirations of individual contributors. There has always tended to be a greater overlap of organizational and individual goals for higher management than for the rank and file. To an extent, this will inevitably persist, and total goal congruence is not to be expected at any level. But effective organizational-development effort can extend the overlap and thereby not only motivate the individual to work toward organizational goals, but also provide him with more satisfaction in his working life. Thus, while our approach seems to emphasize the managerial perspective of obtaining motivation toward organizational goals, it concurrently addresses the issue of providing more psychological rewards for the individual from his work.

# 6
# CONCLUSIONS

This small volume has been addressed to three key developmental issues that face any organization: developing the organization-environment interface, the group-to-group interface, and the organization-individual interface. Without in any way asserting that the three selected issues are all-inclusive or even necessarily more critical than others, we have emphasized and illustrated their central importance. But beyond this we have shown that these three developmental issues can be approached by using a single set of related concepts and tools so that the overall developmental program of any given organization can be handled in a unified manner both in planning and in action. We have consistently emphasized the idea of fitting the organization to its immediate relevant environment and to the characteristics of its individual contributors. This approach is based on the fundamental premise that *there is no one best way to organize;* rather, organizations need to be systematically tailored to collective goals and individual human purposes.

In order to clarify our approach to the development issues at the three selected interfaces, we have in the preceding three chapters described a number of actual experiences in which the authors (or, in a few instances, close colleagues) have been involved. Each of these cases involved an application of behavioral-science tools to problem situations which, to a greater or lesser extent, moved through a complete cycle of change. This final chapter now provides an opportunity to review all these experiences with three different questions in mind.

1. We will consider what light these cases can throw on the general topic of the strategy and tactics of organizational change at any of these interfaces.

2. We will consider some specific and practical issues thus raised for practicing managers.

3. We will look at some broader issues involving the shaping of contemporary organizations to better serve the present needs of society and of the individual.

## THE ORGANIZATIONAL-CHANGE PROCESS

Throughout our case examples we trust that we have demonstrated the importance of systematic diagnosis in approaching developmental problems in organizations. We have seen that problems in the three interfaces present themselves to the attention of management by a wide variety of symptoms. It is the work of analysis and diagnosis to translate these symptoms into a coherent picture on the basis of which action can be planned and carried out with a reasonable assurance that objectives will be achieved. It is the work of diagnosis to sort out the multiple causes of a developmental problem and to place specific phenomena in a systematic framework. This is the part of the change process that serves to avoid superficial and premature action. Once a reasonably complete diagnosis is developed, it in itself tends to induce the next necessary steps: specifying the desired direction of change and identifying the more promising variables which should be altered to allow the organization to move in the desired direction.

To be more specific, we have seen examples of the employment of both some particular concepts and some measurement instruments to aid the diagnostic process. These tools, taken together, provide for the selection and collection of relevant data, and then help in ordering the data so that an overall view of the issue is developed, on the basis of which action-planning can proceed. The cases cited have indicated a good deal of variety in the degree to which quantification was used in assessing organization facts. We varied our use of quantification depending upon the receptiveness of the organization to the use of such instruments. Some companies have had a bad history with such methods, while in others the procedure is so unfamiliar that it might stir up more anxiety than the results would justify. In these instances, other, less precise, methods were used: semistructured interviews and/or meetings with a focus on producing a composite diagnosis.

No matter which method was employed to generate a diagnosis, the results in all cases were fed back to the relevant participants. The feedback was not of raw data but rather of data organized within a conceptual framework. Time was provided to discuss, modify, and generally digest both the data and the concepts so that a more generally accepted diagnosis emerged. The object of these feedback sessions was therefore twofold— both to obtain a reasonable consensus on the facts and a shared way of thinking and talking about these facts. In the feedback sessions we have conducted, the data have in fact generally meshed with the managers' own personal experiences. The concepts we have used in organizing the data have generally proved to "make sense" to them: they have fitted the managers' intuitive ways of thinking.

The process of creating a shared diagnosis blends into the next change step of developing an action plan. Several of the cases illustrate this overlapping of diagnosis and planning. Action-planning usually involves alternate periods of exploring "what is desirable" and examining "what is," so that the resulting plan represents a practical method for closing the gap between the two. Throughout our cases we have emphasized the examination of multiple variables or "levers" that can induce changes in the organization, to close the gap between the status quo and the desired state.

In the organization-environment interface, we saw a variety of cases of mismatching between the actual features of organizational units and their desired state as deduced from an analysis of the characteristics of their relevant sector of the environment. Depending upon the size and nature of the mismatch or gap, different change methods were employed. The cases described in respect to the group-to-group interface and the organization-individual interface presented parallel issues of action-planning. In each case, a careful effort was made to tailor the change methods to the nature of the gap between the actual and the desired. The change methods used have included a variety of structural and procedural changes, such as change in the formal communication and control procedures, change in goal-setting procedures, change in the authority structure and division of labor, change in the selection criteria. In addition, a variety of educational designs have been employed, including variants of sensitivity training and of the case method of instruction. In many instances, combinations of change methods were employed. For example, in Chapter 3 we saw an instance of a combination of structural and

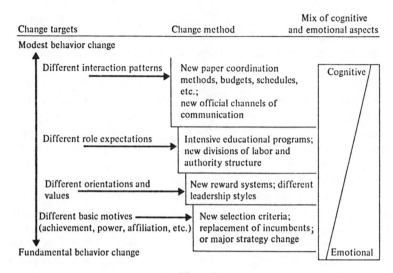

**Figure 6**

educational interventions in the heavy industrial firm concerned with fitting its dispersed plants to environmental differences. In Chapter 4 we cited an example of blending the data feedback from a quantified diagnostic study with an educational simulation exercise and a "differentiation laboratory." In Chapter 5 we described a combination of systematic data feedback with an educational program designed to alter the leadership style of key managers.

It is dangerous to generalize about the selection of change methods, but the general guideline holds that one matches the method to the amount of behavior change that is needed to close the gap. As the amount of desired behavior change increases, one can add additional change methods to secure the desired end results. Figure 6 indicates the increasing complexity and difficulty of effecting behavior changes as one moves from a desire to alter customary interaction patterns in an organization to shifting role expectations, changing values and orientations (such as toward time), to the most stubborn variable: changing basic motives. The parallel array of change methods is suggestive of the way methods can be added to match the difficulty of the desired change target. It also suggests that, as the depth of change increases, the process involved shifts from being primarily a cognitive one to being primarily an emotional one.

This way of addressing the planning of change avoids a number of dilemmas that stall many change efforts. All too often, change efforts become bogged down in a fruitless debate about whether it is better to employ structural methods or educational methods. Another version of this debate is whether things change people or people change things. A third version is whether attitude changes precede or follow changes in behavior. Even the oldest controversy of them all, heredity *vs.* environmental influences, still consumes a vast amount of time and energy. These all become dead issues with this way of thinking about change. The needless debate is converted into the practical planning of the appropriate mix of methods needed to close the gap between the actual and desired state of affairs.

An additional planning argument that is completely bypassed by this way of thinking is the question of what is the one best way to organize, to control, to reward, etc. These discussions are no longer relevant since the desired model is conditional on the task to be done, the environmental conditions to be handled, and the characteristics of the individual contributors involved. It follows that it takes different kinds of organizations to deal with these different realities. So, once the broad strategy of the organization for conducting environmental transactions is reasonably clear, and the needs of members are understood, the rest of the planning can proceed without these particular kinds of debilitating arguments. Structures and procedures are designed to be consistent with each major organizational task and not necessarily with one another.

The planning of the action phase is apt to blend into and overlap with the action-implementation phase. This is true for two reasons. First of all, action-planning logically includes planning the sequence and timing of action steps. The resulting schedule creates a followup mechanism for taking progress readings at predetermined check points. The action phase is in this sense simply an extension of the planning sequence. Second, the key to effective implementation is, of course, the degree of commitment to the change felt by certain key participants who must implement it. While an organization can afford to have some members who will comply with the new requirements with but faint enthusiasm and a very few who are in active opposition, most of the key figures need both understanding and emotional commitment if important and lasting change is to be effected. This understanding and commitment needs to be built during the diagnostic and planning phases. If it is achieved at these stages, the implementation will predictably go relatively smoothly. Several of the cases indicated the advantages gained at the implementation phase when key people affected were involved in the planning process and developed understanding and commitment at that time. The implementation phase was, in effect, well started before the planning was complete.

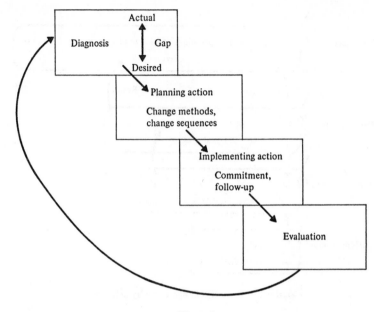

**Figure 7**

Thus, if each phase of the planning cycle is well executed, it both eases the accomplishment of the next phase and speeds it up so that the complete cycle can be executed in a shorter time span. Figure 7 diagrams this sequence and the possibility of overlapping phases. It also indicates how the final phase of evaluation really consists of a return to the first diagnostic phase.

We have stressed the utility of the concepts of differentiation and integration as aids to understanding developmental issues. This has led us to attend primarily to the way organizations are differentiated into subsystems which then need to be integrated with their environmental sector and with each other. In addition to helping us understand these lateral relations in organizations, the same two concepts can also help us clarify the relations between different echelons in a complex organization and how they play their differentiated roles in the change process. It is well known by common observation and by research that the top echelons of organization tend to have longer-term planning horizons, and the lower echelons a short range. This form of differentiation of task between echelons is one clue to a well-run organization. The integration takes place as the planning work at the top echelon provides guidelines for the lower echelons to use in defining desired states. In turn, the evaluation data from

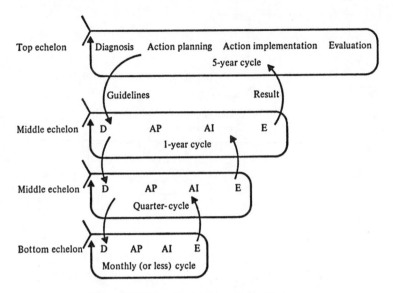

**Figure 8** Schematic change cycle by echelons.

the lower echelons provides inputs upward to the diagnostic phase of the longer change cycle. This integrating linkage proceeds at each echelon, as is schematically shown in Fig. 8. Following out this idea, each echelon, including the lowest, can theoretically be included as participants to a degree in a complete change cycle. Each group will be developing plans centered around the information to which they have the best access.

## ISSUES FOR MANAGERS

At the outset of this book we indicated that it would be primarily addressed to the manager, and would focus on the need to increase his understanding of organizations and thus enhance his ability to control and direct them in response to human purposes. While one could argue that this is necessary and important for persons in a variety of roles in our society, it is clearly of crucial importance to the persons in managerial roles within organizations. It is for this reason that we have consistently slanted this book towards persons who now occupy or aspire to occupy such positions. We believe that the concepts for and approaches to organizational development, which we have described, offer managers the greatest probability of being able to develop their organization so that it can accomplish its particular goals, while at the same time it meets the needs of individual contributors. However, using the tools and concepts we have been discussing will pose for managers a number of practical problems that we will review below.

While the systemic view of organizations which we have been describing seems to us to offer the best approach to dealing with organization-development issues, there is no question that it is more complex than other views of organizations. For example, it is far simpler to view organizations in terms of the universal prescriptions developed by early management theorists who have been labelled the "classicists" such as Fayol, Mooney, and Urwick. If one follows their prescriptions to the letter, there is only "one best way" to organize. It is not necessary to understand the requirements of different tasks, nor the complex issues raised by the varying needs of different sets of organization members. All one has to do is understand these principles and apply them. The temptation to follow this simpler approach is obviously great; and we must admit that even our own evidence suggests that for organizations faced with stable and uniform environments this approach makes a great deal of sense.[1] But one problem, as many of the examples used in the previous chapters illustrate, is that a great many organizations are faced with dynamic and uncertain environments where the classical principles of management do not work at all well. In addition, even in those situations where this approach makes sense, there are often other human and task factors which must be taken into account.

The classical approach, however, is not the only relatively simple and universal one available. More recently some behavioral scientists have argued for what we might term "participative" approaches.[2] It is worthy of note in this connection that the late Douglas McGregor, whose work many would place in this camp, argued in his last book, *The Professional Manager*, for a sociotechnical systems approach, not unlike the one we have proposed.[3] This participative approach, like the classical one, offers a fairly clearcut prescription of how best to organize. It is relatively simple and provides a single set of principles to follow. But its shortcoming, like that of the classical approach, is that it makes certain simplifying

1    P. R. Lawrence and J. W. Lorsch, *Op. cit.*

2    R. Likert, *The Human Organization: Its Management and Value.* New York: McGraw-Hill, 1967.

3    D. McGregor, *The Professional Manager.* New York: McGraw-Hill, 1967.

assumptions about individual needs and also fails to recognize the other fact which we have stressed: that different task or environmental requirements at any of these three interfaces require different organizational characteristics.

Thus, these two approaches, although offering different prescriptions, are both simpler than the systemic tools we are advocating. They do not take account of the full complexity of the issues at each of the interfaces we have discussed. As a result, attempts to apply them without modifying them for the specific situational demands have at times been unsuccessful. For example, Greiner, in his survey of organization-change studies, lists among "less successful" change patterns one which was based on the participative approach and some based on the classical approach. In these instances and others which we could cite from our own experience, the desired changes in the organization did not occur, because the managers and/or the consultants were proceeding with a set of concepts which were inadequate to clarify the organization-development issues with which they were confronted. To make these efforts successful, the managers and consultants would have had to take into account other factors in the situation outside the parameters of their simpler and universalistic prescriptions. We would argue that the complexity which the systemic approach explicitly takes into account would also have to be dealt with, at least implicitly, if these other approaches are to be successfully applied. By explicitly building task and individual differences into the concepts we utilize, we feel we have less chance of missing important factors as we attack OD problems. It is not that we like complex concepts, but that the real organizational world *is* complex and is so at each interface.

Nevertheless, the initial point still holds: these concepts are complex. At each interface we are asking the manager interested in organizational development to understand and deal with a complex set of interrelationships between task requirements and individual needs, and among these and formal organizational variables. Further, while we have treated the organization-environment, group-to-group, and individual-organization interfaces separately, it is clear that in practice issues at all these interfaces become intermingled. When one deals with a problem at the individual-organization interface (such as our example of the sales force marketing medical-technology products; see Chapter 5), it will often be necessary to change formal control and reward procedure, which in turn will alter the orientations and behavioral styles of the individual contributors involved. Altering these variables means we are also changing the state of differentiation in the organization, hopefully toward a situation where a particular unit can deal more effectively with its environmental interface. A change in the state of differentiation as we work on the organization-environment interface, also will affect the integration achieved at the group-to-group interface. For example, in the new-products division mentioned in Chapter 3, when the differentiation between the sales and development groups was altered so that they were no longer competing for relations with the same environmental sector, it was possible to improve the relations between these groups. While these are only a few examples of the interrelations between these interfaces, they clearly point to another source of the complexity in organization-development work.

Thus OD work at each interface is complex, and is further complicated by the interrelationship among these three interfaces, as well as other interfaces we have not considered in detail (e.g., the person-to-person interface within a work group). Our answer to this complexity, as we have suggested throughout the book, is that managers should use concepts which are adequate to deal with it, rather than overly simplistic ones like the classical and participative approaches. This does create a problem, however, if we recognize the pragmatic fact that most top managers, who are in a position to initiate OD activities, are extremely busy and also are preoccupied with complex marketing, financial, operational, and/or strategic problems. Given these time pressures and the overload on managers' cognitive and emotional apparatus, how can they also find the time and energy to use these systemic tools to deal with complex organization-development issues? Might it not make more sense to select simpler approaches to organization problems?

One answer to this sort of question lies in looking at the ways in which competent managers deal with the complexity of other problems with which they are confronted, in the financial or marketing area, for example. They obviously do not opt for overly simple analytic schemes in these areas. Rather they rely on analytic tools which can help them order the complexity with which they are confronted. This is what we believe they must also do with organization-development problems. The constraint of time and limited cognitive capacity on these external problems is handled by top managers in at least two complementary ways. First, they often engage internal or external specialists who are skilled in financial or marketing analysis to study the problem in depth, and to order the complexity, so that they can use their time more economically to make decisions. Second, along with the first approach, they gain a familiarity with the necessary analytic tools themselves, so that they can use them on their own and so that they can understand the specialists' ideas. These are the two complementary approaches which we feel also hold promise of helping managers use the analytic tools we have been discussing to develop their organizations. We now want to examine some of the issues connected with applying these methods to OD problems.

## TWO COMPLEMENTARY APPROACHES TO ORGANIZATION-DEVELOPMENT ACTIVITY

In considering these two methods for assisting managers to cope with the complexity of organization-development issues, it is useful to start by looking at the role a specialist group can play. By beginning here, we can summarize some of the important aspects of the OD process and assess their impact on the use of specialists to work on these particular problems.

On the surface, proposing the creation of a group of specialists to work on organization-development issues does seem to make as much sense as creating groups of specialists to work on problems of computer applications, operations research, market research, long-range planning, financial analysis, etc. But a review of several of the factors we have previously mentioned as critical to success in OD activity indicates that the creation and use of specialized organization-development groups must be approached with caution.

First, our own work and that of others clearly indicates that effective organizational change is most apt to occur when the top managers of the organization are involved and when they indicate their commitment to the change effort.[4] Related to this, it seems to be important for the individual contributors involved in the change at least to understand the need for change and how the change will be rewarding for them. Beyond this, where feasible, there also appears to be some merit in having many organization members involved in identifying the need for change and in planning the changes.[5] As we have suggested above, this does provide the best promise of obtaining commitment to change. However, to reiterate the other side of the trade-off, it may also mean less sophisticated solutions to organizational problems, since many organization members will not have the conceptual tools or the relevant information to understand these problems or to develop sound solutions to them.

---

4    L. E. Greiner, "Patterns of Organization Change," Harv. Bus. Rev., May-June, 1967.

5    Greiner, *Op. cit.*

Having OD specialists in the organization, working with managers and other members to diagnose problems and plan change, is obviously one way of getting both involvement and more sophisticated solutions. But all of this also points to the problems inherent in using a specialist group of organization-development experts. Somehow, they must be closely tied to the various top managers interested in the development of the organization. These top decision-makers must have confidence in the OD specialists and must be willing to share their concerns about the organization with them. While this seems easy in theory, we have found all too often in practice that in organizations where organization-development specialists already do exist, they are at a level so far removed from the top decision-makers that they cannot effectively relate to them. To be effective, however, the organization-development specialists must also be able to relate to other organization members. This, in our experience to date, is not so much of a problem. Yet if OD specialists become more closely tied to top management (as we feel they must be to be effective), this will create more problems in relating to other organization members. The only solution which we can offer to bridge this gap will be the interpersonal skill of these specialists.

If an OD specialist is going to be effective at achieving both commitment to, and more sophisticated solutions for, organization-development issues, he will have to clearly view his role as that of an educator, and a diagnostician as well as a consultant. That is, he will have to be able to develop techniques for identifying organization problems and analyzing their causes. He will have to be able to educate managers and other organization members in the use of concepts to conduct diagnoses and to plan action. Finally, he will have to act as a consultant in providing his own action proposals for the managers to consider.

To do all of these things he would not have to be a superman, but it would help. He and the management will clearly have to take a broader view of his role than is now usually the case. Today, too often the organization-development specialist is seen by management (and even at times by himself) as a specialist *exclusively in some one technique,* be it managerial grid, T-groups, motivation training, or job enlargement, etc. If he is to effectively perform the multiple activities of educator, diagnostician, and consultant, this view will have to change.

But more than his and others' perceptions of his role must change. He will need broader training in the behavioral sciences, particularly in the kind of systemic tools we have been discussing, if he is to be effective. In fact, as we have suggested, his knowledge will have to be sufficient to educate other members of the organization to the meaning and use of these concepts.

The question of educating other members of the organization to the use of these concepts brings us to the other complementary approach to improving the capacity within an organization to deal with its developmental issues. We have seen that one set of members whom the OD specialist can and must educate is top management. In making this statement, we should emphasize that we are not implying that top managers are ignoramuses on organizational affairs; but we do protest that, given the time pressures they face and their broad interest in the multiple facets of the business, they need help in understanding organizational issues and particularly in keeping pace with the contributions which the rapidly developing behavioral and organizational sciences can make to the solution of organizational problems.

One approach we are aware of which organization-development specialists have already taken in educating their top managers is what we might call an "OD laboratory." This type of program consists of a series of uninterrupted sessions of the top management group, each of which lasts two or three days. By the top management group we mean those managers at the top of the organization in question, whether it be a company, a major product department, or a functional unit. The objective of these sessions is to give members of this group a chance to review their own functions as well as to consider issues in the larger organization. In the cases where we have observed or been involved in these laboratories, they seem to emanate from the concerns of top management and their internal OD specialists about unresolved organizational problems which require attention. While the first session often concentrates on a review by the top group of its own internal operations and processes, subsequent sessions are devoted to an inventory of organization-wide problems. In some of the cases we have in mind, this inventory was built from the manager's own assessment of the organization. In other cases, such as that of the plastics organization described in Chapter 4, the assessment was provided through a formal diagnostic study, conducted by the internal OD specialist, with the collaboration of an outside consultant.

Through the early stages of these laboratories, the organization-development specialist acts as an educator, in the sense that he educates managers about the process within their group. Where the managers are trying to identify organizational problems themselves, he can facilitate this process by feeding in comments and/or data which help them to more fully understand all the dimensions of the problem and not just the obtrusive symptoms which they observe. In those cases where an explicit diagnostic study of the organization has been conducted, the organization-development specialist carries out a similar educational function. By explaining the concepts used to organize the presentation for data feedback, he educates the managers to a way of thinking about the organization. In our own experience, employing the concepts of differentiation and integration, we have found that the managers not only use them to understand the particular problem at hand, but also retain an understanding for application to other problems. We suspect that the same would hold true for the other concepts we have used.

Once the managers have arrived at a diagnosis of the situation which they accept, the later sessions of the OD laboratory can be devoted to identifying solutions and working them out. During this phase, the organization-development specialist contributes through interjecting his own ideas and also, if necessary, by arranging more explicit conceptual inputs. The latter is often necessary because, as the managers begin to search for solutions to problems, they want better conceptual tools with which to evaluate and understand the consequences of different alternatives. To provide this input, the OD specialist can rely on readings and/or outside experts. When we have been involved in the latter role, we have found it useful not only to use lectures and discussions of the concepts in the abstract, but also to spend time on the discussion of teaching cases drawn from parallel situations in other organizations. This enables the managers to grasp the concepts and to apply them in situations where their emotional involvement is lower and analytic objectivity is easier. Then, with a better understanding of how to apply the concepts, they can return to their own problems.

These organization-development laboratories (or a process like them, regardless of the label it is given), we feel, offer one method the OD specialist can use to educate managers. From our point of view, this approach has several distinct advantages. First, it provides the top management group with an educational opportunity to learn a set of concepts they can take with them and build on to solve the recurring organizational issues with which they will be faced. Second, it obviously provides a chance to examine, at least in a preliminary way, their own working relationships and how they are related to wider organizational problems. This approach also is one way of resolving the dilemma between getting managerial commitment to some acceptable solution and the development of a more sophisticated solution. Through these laboratory sessions, the top managers will hopefully become committed to a solution which is based on a sound conceptual framework. As they work on their own immediate problems, they also learn to use the sort of complex conceptual scheme we have been describing throughout this book. Obviously, these sessions do not automatically solve the problem of getting commitment at other levels of the organizations. However, they do provide an opportunity for the top managers to confront this issue and to consider how best to implement their preferred solution and still achieve organizational commitment to it.

Before leaving these two approaches to helping managers deal with the complexity of organization-development issues, it may be useful to say a few words about the role of outside consultants in relation to the internal OD specialist and his role as an educator. Our own experience has made us acutely aware of the fact that organization-development problems are so complex and so persistent that an external consultant by himself can play only a limited role in helping managers solve them. As we have suggested through our examples in the earlier chapters, an outside consultant can be useful as a diagnostician, as an educator, and as a proposer of solutions for specific problem situations. But constant reliance on a consultant by management should be a warning signal that something is missing in their own resources for maintaining the health of the organization, for organization development is not a one-shot treatment. Rather, it is a constant and continuing process, in which the management of any organization must consistently engage. Outside consultants can provide new approaches and tools from time to time, but in the final analysis the capacity for organization-development must reside inside the organization. It is for this reason that we have placed so much emphasis on the role of internal OD specialists, and upon educating managers in the use of the behavioral-science tools available to help them work on organization-development issues.

## ORGANIZATION AND THE WIDER SOCIETY

Throughout this book we have stressed the idea of thinking of organizations as tools to be adapted to their respective environmental tasks and the general needs of their contributors. This emphasis creates a somewhat technocratic flavor to our approach to organization development. To caricature it: measure up the task and we will grind out a custom-fitted organization. Is this simply a time-and-motion study grown large? What has happened to the flesh-and-blood people? Where will a bevy of "tailored organizations" tend to take a society? These are reasonable questions that we will address in closing, even though our answers can be only fragmentary.

Organizations are central facts of modern life. They serve as crucial mediators between the individual and the entire society. They are engulfed in the tension between our purposes as unique individuals and our collective goals as members of communities of men. In placing importance on thinking of organizations as tools, we are joining others in the task of demystifying these pivotal institutions. Men tend to assume, other things being equal, that the organization with which they first have intimate contact represents some universal approach, expecially in regard to basic matters such as authority, decision-making, communication, and control procedures. These are the very elements which need to be seen as variables if organizations are to be designed on a coherent basis. These basic assumptions, often only implicit in our behavior in organizations, need to be made explicit to free people so that they may choose between a wider array of alternatives. Our knowledge of the matching process between organizational variables and tasks, environmental conditions, and human predispositions clearly needs extending. But, as it grows, it opens an exciting prospect. Some of these possibilities can be seen by reflecting on the many forms of criticism that are now directed at organizations.

Organizations are pervasively described these days as too impersonal, too big, as being beyond control by mere mortals. They are even seen by some as monsters which man has created but which seem to have acquired wills of their own. The antidote to this type of thinking is to better understand organizations as tools to serve man's individual and collective purposes. In a similar vein, organizations are often seen as repressing man's creative capacities. This fear is based on the assumption that all organizations are rigid bureaucracies full of petty rules that reward conformity much more than innovation. In visualizing an organization as a tool, we can immediately see that such an organization is only one of many types. It may be suitable in circumstances where regularity of task performance outweighs all other considerations, but a person with strong creative talents would, of course, avoid such an organization. The point is that, as organizations or parts of organizations become better tailored to their tasks, individuals can increasingly select their work roles on the basis of individual preferences, secure in the knowledge that the associated organizational disciplines will be task-based rather than arbitrary. People can express themselves and their interests through task performance with a minimum of unnecessary organizational interference.

Another line of contemporary comment portrays organizations as centers of vast power which heavily influence the lives of ordinary people in ways beyond their control. Certainly top managers and large stockholders of business organizations have above-average power—to argue otherwise would be ridiculous. But, as more and more aspects of organizational affairs become subject to systematic analysis, top-management becomes constrained in its decisions by the knowledge that its behavior is subject to scrutiny. For managers to act on personal whims becomes increasingly costly in a measurable way. The realm of decisions about organizational form and process is one of the few areas of organizational life where strictly personal preferences of senior people can still be imposed upon others in an arbitrary fashion. Better knowledge of organizations as tools, if generally available, will tend to constrain and discipline this one area of personal power. Professionals and middle- and lower-level managers can have a more rational basis for arguing for needed organizational change and a sounder basis for making personal career decisions.

A final line of current comment centers on the materialistic emphasis of American life. This feature of our society is usually seen by commentators as a widely-shared character defect. But here we would argue that it is more specifically a resultant of our organizational life than is generally recognized. Business organizations are geared to maximize the value of material abundance, and anyone who argues that hunger is a sin places value on material abundance. We would submit that, as a culture, we have made our most striking advances in organizational innovation in the business sector during the last century. Aside from the obviously great impact of the physical sciences, this organizational innovation in business must have contributed to the vast material productivity of our industry. Certainly the fact that Europeans are switching analysis of their productivity gap *vis à vis* the United States from a "technology gap" to a "managerial gap" is witness to this interpretation. Therefore, we would suggest that we, as a people, are known as "materialistic" partly because we have been comparatively more successful in creating effective organizational forms in the business area than we have been in developing organizations geared to other purposes. Perhaps better knowledge of organizations as tools will in time give us the power to make comparable advances in social innovation among organizations oriented primarily to other tasks and values. The cases cited in this book were all drawn from business organizations for the obvious reason that this is where our experience lies. But the ideas and approaches described lend themselves to testing for their relevance to other kinds of organizations. Certainly there is no theoretical limit to the relevance of organization development as a growing field of knowledge and practice relevant to organizations of all types. To the extent that such an endeavor meets with success, both the purposes of individuals as individuals and those human values we must seek on a collective basis can be served. The better we can tailor organizations as adaptive, effective tools, the more we can harmonize and reconcile the inevitable tension between our individual and collective purposes. In this way, the idea of tailoring organizations is anything but a sterile technocratic approach. It is instead one path toward the better achievement of pluralistic values.